Computer-Aided Software Engineering

Computer-Aided Software Engineering
the methodologies, the products, and the future

Chris Gane

Rapid System Development Inc.

Prentice Hall, Englewood Cliffs, New Jersey 07632

Editorial/production supervision: bookworks
Cover design: Diane Saxe
Manufacturing buyer: Mary Ann Gloriande

 © 1990 by Rapid System Development Inc.
Published by Prentice-Hall, Inc.
A Division of Simon & Schuster
Englewood Cliffs, New Jersey 07632

While all reasonable efforts have been made to supply complete and
accurate information, and to ensure that the procedures given in this book
function as described, the author and Rapid System Development Inc.
present this publication "as is" without warranty of any kind either express or
implied, including, but not limited to, the implied warranties of
merchantability or fitness for a particular purpose, and accept no
responsibility for its use, nor for any infringements of patents or other rights
of third parties which would result.

The publisher offers discounts on this book when ordered in bulk
quantities. For more information write:
   Special Sales/College Marketing
   Prentice-Hall, Inc.
   College Technical and Reference Division
   Englewood Cliffs, NJ 07632

Printed in the United States of America
10 9 8 7 6 5 4 3 2 1

ISBN 0-13-176231-1

Prentice-Hall International (UK) Limited, *London*
Prentice-Hall of Australia Pty. Limited, *Sydney*
Prentice-Hall Canada Inc., *Toronto*
Prentice-Hall Hispanoamericana, S.A., *Mexico*
Prentice-Hall of India Private Limited, *New Delhi*
Prentice-Hall of Japan, Inc., *Tokyo*
Simon & Schuster Asia Pte. Ltd., *Singapore*
Editora Prentice-Hall do Brasil, Ltda., *Rio de Janeiro*

My warmest thanks to all those working on CASE products who have taken time to help me, and to Kati Szabo, who put it all together (yet again).

CONTENTS

Part II: Detailed analysis of EXCELERATOR

Part III: Product summaries

Introduction:

What is CASE?

The acronym CASE is generally used to refer to Computer-Aided Software Engineering, though some writers have tried to extend it to mean Computer-Aided *Systems* Engineering, on the grounds that the field extends beyond the production of just software. The term was coined in the early 1980s, when it became clear that graphical tools like data flow diagrams (DFDs), entity-relationship diagrams (ERDs), and structure charts could help with systems analysis and design. Since aerospace, automobile, and other engineers got great value out of computer-aided design (CAD) systems for developing drawings and doing calculations, it seemed that computer-aided graphics might be similarly helpful to Information Systems professionals. In fact, McDonnell Douglas used their CAD expertise to produce the first product in 1981: STRADIS/DRAW.

It soon become clear, though, that a mere graphics capability was not enough; the diagram objects should be placed in a design database, which could also hold details of data elements and process logic. The system logical model built up in the design database could be tested for completeness and consistency before being printed out to form a system specification. This group of facilities was realized in EXCELERATOR, released in 1984 and described in detail in Part II of this report.

The success of EXCELERATOR really established the CASE market segment; this report describes 17 other products which essentially compete with EXCELERATOR in allowing graphical modelling of systems and the creation of a design database. As the market analysis in Chapter 10 shows, the sales of this group of products, which are referred to variously as modelling tools, analyst/designer workbenches, analysis toolkits, or front-end CASE products, are growing at a rate of some 70% per year, and will soon constitute a billion-dollar software market.

With this success, vendors of other aids to system development, such as data dictionaries, code generators, restructuring tools, and project management packages, have sought to get on the bandwagon and reposition their products as CASE products. Indeed, if software engineering is the discipline of software development and maintenance, and if their products use the computer to aid any part of those activities, they have a perfect right to do so. One may ask, however, where this process should stop. Is a debugger a CASE product? Is a test-data generator a CASE product? To an assembly language programmer, a COBOL compiler could be seen as a CASE product; after all, it uses the computer to aid in the production of software!

This report suggests that the distinguishing characteristic of a CASE product is that it builds within itself a design database, at a higher level than code statements or physical data element definitions. This design database, referred to in the report as a repository, typically holds information about the data to be stored in the system, the business logic of the processes to be implemented, the physical layout of screens and reports, and other requirements/design information. On this definition, it is not necessary to have graphical capability to be a CASE product, though most of the products reviewed here do so.

CASE products are thus a special sub-class of development/maintenance aids. They include code generators and reverse-engineering tools which extract specification-level logic from code. On this definition, programming aids such as code exercisers, debuggers, and test data generators would *not* be classed as CASE tools, since they do not build a design database; nor would restructuring tools which simply translate one set of source statements into a (more readable/changeable) set of source statements.

However the defining lines are drawn, it should be clear from this report that we are dealing with an important, dynamically-growing, new class of software which has a lot to offer in improving the speed, quality, and cost of system development and maintenance.

Structure of the report

As the Contents shows, the report is divided into three parts:

Part I: The methodologies

This section of the report presents each of the main interactive graphical and other techniques supported by some or all CASE tools, with an explanation of where the technique should be used in system development, and of how the techniques fit together.

Logical modelling of data/process
The purpose of logical modelling is to provide a reasonably rapid way for the users and designers of a system to express, exchange, and refine their initial (usually vague) ideas about its scope and content, using diagrams to show the data, the processes (functions), and their inter-relationships. Two main diagram types are used:

- data flow diagrams (DFDs), which show the processes, data stores, and data flows into, around, and out of the system. The Gane/Sarson and Yourdon/DeMarco DFD notations are presented and compared.

- entity-relationship diagrams (ERDs), which show the data entities in the system and the nature of their associations. The Martin, Chen, Ross, and LBMS notations for ERDs are presented and compared.

Other graphical techniques are discussed.

Meta-data repository
DFDs and ERDs show the relationship between data entities and process logic, but do not show the details. Each CASE product needs a place to store the details of data elements, data structures, and process logic, as well as requirements and other textual information. Physical information such as screen/report layout, database definitions, and program logic may be stored in the design database.

Data analysis - normalization
Whether or not the eventual system database will be relational or non-relational, the data structures describing each entity should be expressible in third normal form. Automatable techniques for data analysis are discussed.

Process design
Once the processes/procedures in the system have been identified, some automated aid can be provided in their detailed specification and implementation:

- Screen painting/prototyping
- Action diagrams for expressing the detailed logic to be implemented.
- Structure charts for designing invocation hierarchies of procedural programs; the Yourdon/Constantine and Jackson techniques are presented.

Code generation
Once the data structures have been designed and the logic of a process has been exactly specified, what is involved in automatic generation of code in any desired target language?

Project management
When analysts and programmers are developing systems with a CASE package, much valuable project management data can be captured as a side-benefit. The CASE package provides a shared data store of project information that can be used to record and analyze progress.

Step-by-step approaches
Two main types of step-by-step approaches to developing systems are in use: Information Engineering and Structured Systems Engineering. The report describes each one and discusses the extent to which they are converging.

Part I concludes with a brief overview of the CASE market-place and a discussion of the likely future of this type of software.

Part II: EXCELERATOR

Part II consists of a fairly detailed description of EXCELERATOR, the product whose success has, in many ways, served to establish this market segment.

Part III: Product summaries

This part of the report describes a total of 82 products from 24 vendors, including graphic modelling tools, data dictionaries, design aids, code generators and interfaces to code generators, project management aids, reverse engineering tools, and other associated products.

For each product, the report gives:

- vendor's address and phone number(s).
- the hardware/software platform(s) that support the product.
- the minimum PC configuration, where relevant.
- the first-copy price.

For each product, the report has an entry dealing with:

- the diagram types which the product supports, and whether the diagram symbols and syntax can be modified by the users.
- any significant limitations on the diagrams.
- the objects that can be stored in the Repository (design database).
- how the Repository is integrated with the graphics facility (where relevant), and how it is integrated with mainframe Repositories.
- what provision the product makes for allowing more than one user to share the Repository at a given time.
- the facility for producing reports to analyze the contents of the Repository.
- the facility for prototyping screens and reports.
- the facility for code generation.
- the facility for generating documents in various formats.
- any facility for supporting a project manager.
- any built-in assistance with design, such as an interactive dialog for normalization.
- the vendor's statement of direction.
- figures supplied by the vendor, or gleaned from industry sources, on unit volume and revenues.
- whether the vendor has a user's group.

Computer-Aided Software Engineering

Part I

The methodologies

Chapter 1

Graphical logical modelling of data/process: data flow diagrams

The purpose of a data flow diagram (DFD) is to show, for a business area or a system or part of a system, where the data comes from, where the data goes to when it leaves the system, where the data is stored, what processes transform it, and the interactions between data stores and processes.

Two principal techniques are widely used: that associated with Gane and Sarson (Ref 1-1), and that associated with Yourdon and DeMarco (Ref 1-2). The two techniques are quite similar; the differences between them are discussed in Section 1.3.

1.1 Gane/Sarson DFD technique

Consider this diagram; it shows CUSTOMERS (an external entity, something outside the system) sending in a stream of "Sales orders" along the data flow arrow.

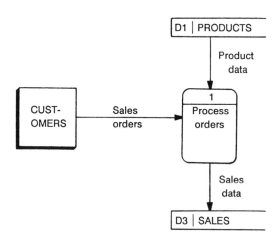

Process 1, "Process orders," handles those orders using information from the data store of PRODUCTS (the elongated rectangle, D1), and puts information about sales into the data store named D3 SALES.

The diagram below shows the whole of the business area, using only the same four symbols. For each sale, Process 1 updates the inventory data store, D2, with the units sold. The data stored in D3 is used by Processes 2 and 3 to prepare bank deposit documents and send them to the bank and to prepare sales reports and send them to management.

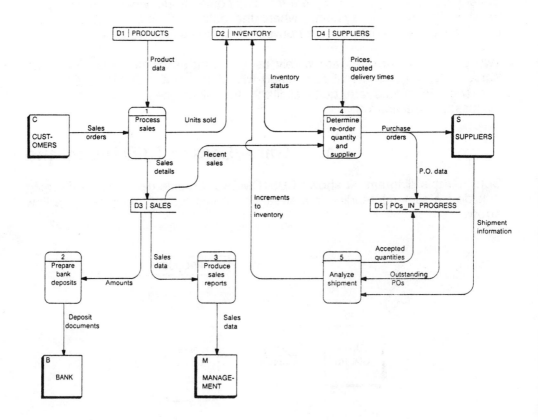

At some appropriate time (notice that timing is not shown on the data flow diagram), Process 4 extracts information about the inventory status of various products and combines it with information from D3 about their past sales, to determine whether a product needs to be reordered. If so, based on information in D4, which describes the prices and delivery times quoted by suppliers, Process 4 chooses the best supplier to order from.

Purchase orders (POs) are sent out to the external entity SUPPLIERS and information about each PO is stored in D5: POS_IN_PROGRESS. When (again at some later time) a shipment is received from a supplier, Process 5 is used to analyze it, extracting data from POS_IN_PROGRESS, to see whether what has been received is what was ordered, incrementing the inventory with the accepted amount, and storing the accepted quantities in the POS_IN_PROGRESS data store.

Note the things that this (DFD) achieves:

1.   The DFD sets a boundary to the area of the system and the area of the business covered by the system. Things which are represented by the external entity symbol (in this case, customers, the bank, managers, and suppliers) are, by definition, outside the system.

    Processes that are not shown on the DFD are not part of the project. For example, the diagram shows the receipt of shipments from suppliers, but not the handling of invoices received from them. This implies that "Accounts Payable" is outside the scope of the project. (This DFD is clearly not complete, by the way; there is no provision for updating PRODUCTS and SUPPLIERS, for example.)

2.   The DFD is non-technical. There is nothing shown on a DFD that is not easily understandable to business people who are familiar with the business area depicted, whether or not they know anything about computers.

    Since the DFD's symbols are non-physical, it shows the underlying logical essence of the information system, and therefore is highly meaningful to business people whether or not they know anything about computers. After a minute or two's explanation of the symbols, anyone who can read a map can read a data flow.

Note that the word "logical" has two meanings. It can mean "according to the rules of logic," or, as used here, it can mean "describing the underlying essence of something."

3.   The DFD shows both the data stored in the system and the processes which transform that data. It shows the relationship between the data in the system and the processes in the system. (As we've noted, it doesn't show timing, but that's an important simplification.)

DFD object symbols

External entities   (EEs)   (also called source/sinks,   source/destinations, external agents)

Gane/Sarson's conventional symbol for an EE is a square given solidity by shading on two sides. Often the external entity is given an identifying letter: M for Management, C for Customers, and so on.

External entities are sources and/or destinations of flows of data into and out of the system. They are, by definition, outside the system under consideration. It's helpful to consider the external entity as being "behind a hole in a wall." That is to say, the system knows nothing about what is going on in the external entity.   Data comes into the system through the hole in the wall;   what happened to it before it came into the system does not concern us.   Data from the system goes back through the hole in the wall and disappears;   we are not concerned with what becomes of it.   Data comes into the system only from external entities; it goes out of the system only to external entities.

If, as an analyst, you find yourself describing what goes on inside an external entity, you need to recognize that your system boundary really is wider than you are presently considering.

The external entity may be physically represented by a group of people, such as customers, or perhaps by a system, such as a payroll system. It may be just one person: the President or Comptroller.

Sometimes, for clarity, it's necessary to duplicate external entities to prevent long data flow arrows going from one side of a diagram to another.   This is conventionally done by putting a diagonal stroke in the bottom right-hand corner of the external entity symbol, which says to the reader of the diagram, "There is more than one of this entity."

On very large diagrams, it may be convenient to put a number inside the triangle to show how many instances of the entity there are.   Of course, if this is done, and then another instance of the symbol is added, all the numbers in all the instances of the symbol will need to be updated.

Data flows

Unlike an arrow on a conventional flowchart, which shows the transfer of control from one program step or module to another, the arrow on a DFD is to be thought of as a pathway, down which one or more data structures may pass as some unspecified time.   The timing of the flow of data and the operation of the processes is dealt with in the specification of the processes themselves.   A data flow diagram resembles a railroad map; it shows where the train tracks are laid, but it does not give the time tables.

Usually each data flow arrow has a name which describes only one data structure.   Sometimes, several similar data structures may be shown passing down the same data flow, as shown here:

Some CASE products allow multiple data structures to be associated with a single data flow arrow; others do not.

Branching arrows mean that the same data flow is going from one origin to two different places, as shown in this example:

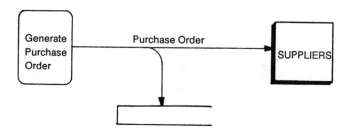

Purchase orders are being sent to suppliers, and the same data is being stored in a data store.

As a general rule, a DFD has more clarity if the data flows go only horizontally and vertically, with curved corners; however, diagonal arrows may be drawn when it is clearer to do so.

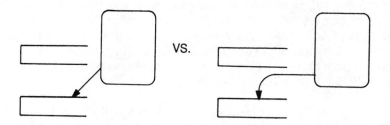

Where data flows cross without meeting, either a hoop (jumping over) or a gap (tunnelling under) may be used.

Data stores

A data store, the symbol for which is an elongated rectangle, is chosen to represent a place where data is necessarily stored in the system; this may be a manual or computer file, or one or more tables in a relational database.

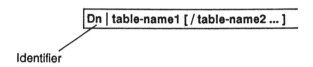

Identifier

Each data store is given an identifier, usually in the form Dnn, e.g. D6.

Data stores may be duplicated to avoid tangled data flows. The symbol for duplication is a triangle added to the left-hand end of the data store symbol. As with external entities, on a large diagram the number of instances of the data store may be given in the triangle:

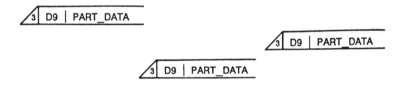

Search arguments

When data is retrieved from a data store, it is usually on the basis of some condition.

SELECT * FROM CUSTOMERS WHERE CUST_ID = 'A94706'

is a SQL statement which will retrieve all the data for the specified customer. The value of CUST_ID, A94706, is the *search argument.*

It is important for the database designer to know all the search arguments that are likely to be used, for example, on each table in a relational database, since each such data element is a candidate for the creation of an index.

Search arguments may be shown on a DFD like this:

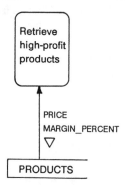

Single-inflow, single-outflow data stores

If any data store has only one flow going into it and only one flow coming out of it, then it should be examined to see whether the storage of data is logically necessary for a business reason, or whether the data store exists only to represent a temporary physical file which functions essentially as a data communications medium.

For example, a floppy disk that is created to carry data from branch office to head office does not represent a storage of data which is logically necessary for the business; the data could be transferred over a telephone line. The floppy disk in this case is just a temporary physical file being used for data transfer. On the other hand, a floppy disk holding details of customers with poor credit ratings, which are held until the Credit Manager has an opportunity to review them, *would* be logically necessary to reflect the way the business is conducted, even though it has only one inflow and one outflow.

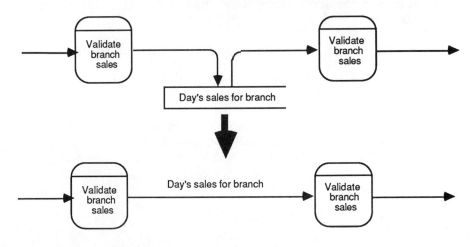

Processes

A process or function that transforms data in some way is normally represented by a rectangle with rounded corners, as shown in the diagram.

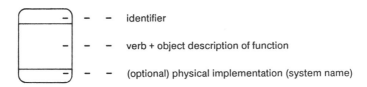

The upper portion of the symbol normally carries an identifying number.

The body of the symbol should have a description of the function of the process, starting with a verb, and followed by an object clause, such as "Generate" (the verb) "sales transactions" (the object clause).

The lower portion may, optionally, contain the department or the program or some other agent which physically implements the process in the system.

What lies behind a process symbol?

As a general rule, error and exception flows should not be shown on a system-wide DFD unless they are very significant to the user community. The system-wide DFD is intended as a working planning tool, not a comprehensive specification: The aim is to show the normal flow of normal data. Error and exception handling should be deferred until the details of procedure units are specified.

It is often useful to have a one- or two-paragraph description of each process that can easily be referred to while reading a DFD. This "process summary" may be stored in the CASE tool's Repository. To state the full logic of a process usually requires one or more pages of Structured English or pseudo-code, as set out in Chapter 6 on "Process Design."

DFD Syntax

CASE products typically generate warning messages if an incorrect entry is made on a DFD, or refuse to accept the erroneous entry, either on-line as the diagram is being changed, or in an analysis report when the diagram is submitted for entry to the Repository.

Syntax rules which can be verified by software

1.   Do all objects (external entries, processes, and data stores) have identifiers?

2.   Do all objects and data flows have names?

3.   Do all processes and data stores have at least one inflow and one outflow?
     If not, why not?

4.   Do all data flows start or end with a process?
     If not, what makes them happen? Data flows from external entities direct to data stores or to other external entities are not correct.

5.   Do all data flows have a directional arrow?

Syntax rules which cannot be (easily) verified by software

6.   Do all data flows have a meaningful name?

7.   Do all processes have a description with the structure "Verb + Noun-clause object?"

8.   Do all data stores represent objects or events of interest?
     If not, can the developer explain their contents?

9.   Are there any data stores with only one inflow and one outflow which are temporary physical intermediate files?

10. Are duplications of symbols kept to a minimum, consistent with having an acceptable number of data flow lines crossing one another?

Note that while some of these criteria (e.g. all data flows starting or ending on a process) can be detected by CASE software and either be disallowed, or be allowed but with a warning message, others do not lend themselves so easily to machine-processing. Thus a CASE tool can flag any data flow arrows with no names, but cannot decide whether existing names are meaningful.

The External Entity/Input/Output (EEIO) listing.

Except where a DFD is very simple, Gane/Sarson recommends starting the development of a DFD by producing an EEIO listing. This simply identifies what you believe are the external entities of the system, and lists the inputs that you know come from them, together with the outputs that you know will go to them.

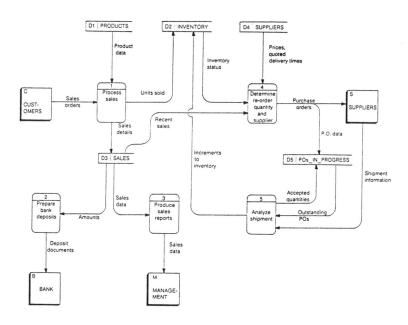

Taking the DFD shown here (the one used earlier in this chapter), the EEIO listing would look like this:

External Entity	Input from EE	Output to EE
CUSTOMERS	Sales orders	
BANK		Deposit documents
MANAGEMENT		Sales data
SUPPLIERS	Shipment information	Purchase orders

(In practice, of course, the list would be much longer.)

1.2   Yourdon/DeMarco DFD technique

The Yourdon/DeMarco technique uses different symbols from Gane/Sarson, as shown here:

Object	Gane/Sarson symbol	Yourdon/DeMarco symbol
	Solidified square	Plain square
External entity		
	Arrow 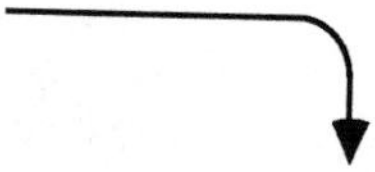	Arrow, may have irregular curve 
Data flow		
	Open-ended rectangle	Parallel lines
Data store		
	Rectangle with rounded corners 	Circle 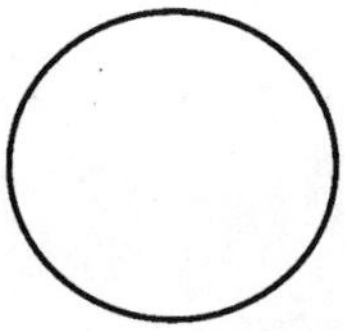
Process		

Thus, the DFD on page 1-2, if expressed in Yourdon/DeMarco notation, might look like this:

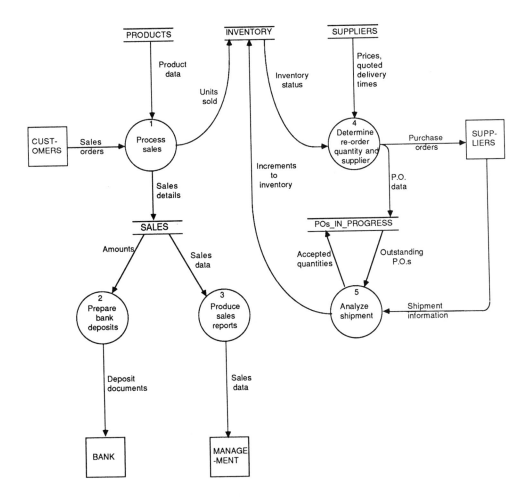

The Yourdon/DeMarco technique suggests that the diagramming of a system should begin with a "context diagram," which simply shows the external entities, inputs to, and outputs from the system or business area. For the DFD on the preceding page, the context diagram would look like this:

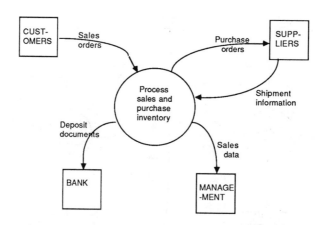

Compare the information shown here with Gane/Sarson's EEIO listing.

Yourdon/DeMarco also strongly recommends that no diagram should have more than seven process "bubbles" on it. Consequently, a significant system needs to be represented by a set of diagrams:

1. a context diagram.

2. a "Level 0" diagram showing the major sub-systems.

3. up to 7 "Level 1" diagrams showing the main functions within each sub-system.

4. up to 49 "Level 2" diagrams showing the details of each function.

It is recommended that functions should be exploded in this way until the details of the process logic or each "primitive" can be written out in a page of Structured English or less. In the case of complex systems, therefore, Level 3 or even Level 4 DFDs may be necessary.

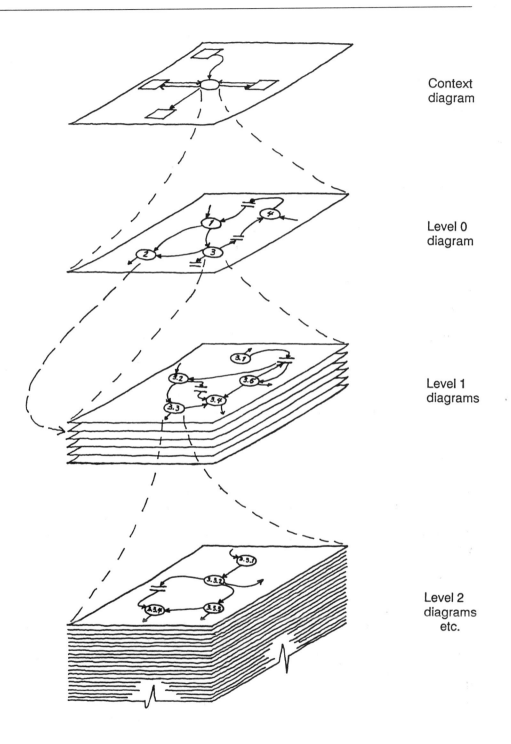

Context
diagram

Level 0
diagram

Level 1
diagrams

Level 2
diagrams
etc.

1.3 Gane/Sarson and Yourdon/DeMarco notations compared

Apart from the question of symbol shape, there are three principal differences between the Gane/Sarson and Yourdon/DeMarco approaches to logical modelling of systems: explosion policy, current system modelling, and relationship of the DFD to the data model.

Explosion policy

As we noted in the previous section, Yourdon/DeMarco strongly recommends that no DFD should have more than seven processes on it, and that complex processes should be exploded until each primitive process on the lowest-level DFD can be documented by a page or less of Structured English, or other form of logic. This implies that a system involving 500 pages of logic (a moderately complex commercial system) would require 70 to 80 linked Yourdon/DeMarco DFDs at different levels of detail to represent it.

Gane/Sarson, on the other hand, while using explosion when necessary, recommends that DFDs should include as many processes and data stores as are practical on any one diagram, and recommends that a single process symbol need not be exploded if it can be documented by 5 to 10 pages of logic. A 500-pages-of-logic system might thus all be shown on a single system-wide DFD with some 100 processes, perhaps on a diagram 17" x 22".

Current system modelling

Usually, when an information system is being planned, it is to replace some currently existing system, which may be automated or manual. This current physical system, however imperfect, is doing some or all of the work that the proposed new physical system is to do. To design the proposed system, we want first to decide on the data and procedures that it must contain; that is, we need to establish a proposed logical system model (one or more DFDs, plus a data model, plus process logic). How is this proposed logical system model to be arrived at?

One way is to establish the details of the current physical system, then abstract from those details to draw a DFD of the current logical system. Then ask, "How does the underlying nature of the current system need to be changed, to solve the problems of the present, and grasp the opportunities of the future?" (Usually, more data has to be captured and stored, and processed more elaborately, quickly, and accurately.) So, the proposed logical model can be derived from the current logical model. Then various possibilities for implementing the proposed logical model can be considered to arrive at a new physical system design. This sequence of steps can be shown diagrammatically:

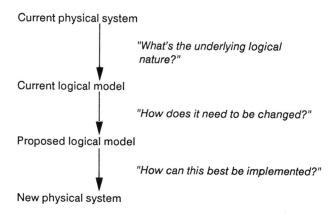

Yourdon/DeMarco recommends carrying out all four steps.

Gane/Sarson takes the position that on each project, a decision has to be made as to whether it is quicker to get to the proposed logical model from the current logical model, or whether it is most productive to say "Forget what we're doing now; in the light of the needs of business, what should the future system do?" and start modelling the proposed system from scratch.

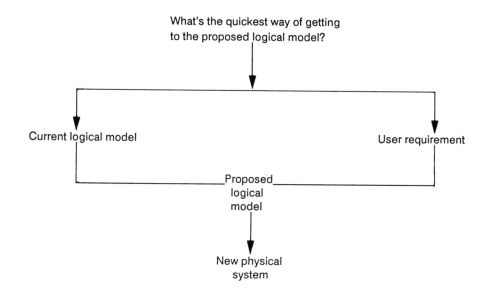

Relationship of the DFD to the data model

Each data flow arrow on a DFD represents a pathway along which data structures (groups of data elements) move into, around, or out of the system. Each data store on a DFD represents a place where one or more data structures are held at rest.   To document the detail that lies behind each DFD, one must specify not only the business logic of each process, but must also specify what data elements are held in each data store and data flow.

Yourdon/DeMarco use a special convention for documenting data structures, allowing for repetition and optionality. So to specify the structure of an invoice containing an invoice number, a customer name/address, an invoice date, possible special instructions, and multiple item lines each with a product code, a quantity, a unit price, and an item cost, Yourdon/DeMarco might write:

Invoice = Invoice-number + Customer-name + Customer-address + Invoice-date
        + (Special instructions)   ( ) means "optional"
        + {Product-code + Quantity + Unit-price + Item-cost}   { } means "repeated"

Gane/Sarson would write the same data structure thus:

Invoice
   Invoice-number
   Customer-name
   Customer-address
   Invoice-date
   [Special instructions]
   *Item-line ***   Hierarchy is shown by
      Product-code   indentation
      Quantity
      Unit-price   [ ]   means "optional"
      Item-cost   *   means "repeated"

Further, Gane/Sarson recommend that all data structures should be reduced to third normal form (for an explanation, see Chapter 5), and that the contents of data stores should be boiled down to one or more related third normal form tables.

Ref 1-1 Gane, C., and Sarson, T.   *Structured Systems Analysis: Tools and Techniques.* Englewood Cliffs, NJ: Prentice-Hall, 1979

Ref 1-2 DeMarco, T.   *Structured Analysis and System Specification.*   Englewood Cliffs, NJ: Prentice-Hall, 1978

Chapter 2

Graphical logical modelling of data:
entity-relationship diagrams

The purpose of an entity-relationship diagram (ERD) is to show the data entities (things of importance to a business area or system about which data needs to be stored) and how they are related to one another.

Note that while a DFD shows both processes and data entities (in the form of data stores), the ERD concentrates just on the data entities. An ERD may also be referred to as a data model diagram.

2.1   Overview

To build up an ERD, we ask first, "What are the entities of interest about which data may need to be stored?" Taking the business dealt with in Chapter 1, the answer might be CUSTOMERS, PRODUCTS, INVENTORY, SUPPLIERS, SALES, and PURCHASE_ORDERS. We create a diagram with a block for each of the entities we have identified. (It is conventional to state the entities as singular nouns; for example, CUSTOMER, rather than CUSTOMERS.) Next we ask, looking at each pair of entities on the diagram, "What, if any, relationships exist between them?"

For example, we know that one customer may be associated with many sales, but each sale can only be for one customer. This is conventionally shown by a line with an arrowhead against the "many" block, as shown here:

(Other notations are discussed in Section 2.5.)

Taking PRODUCT and SALE, one product may be associated with many sales; likewise, one sale may be for many products (at least one, possibly more). In this case, the relationship is shown by a line with an arrowhead on both ends. On the other hand, each product is associated with only one inventory record, and each inventory record is associated with only one product. Consequently, they are joined with a simple line. Adding in all the relationships we can identify gives a diagram like this:

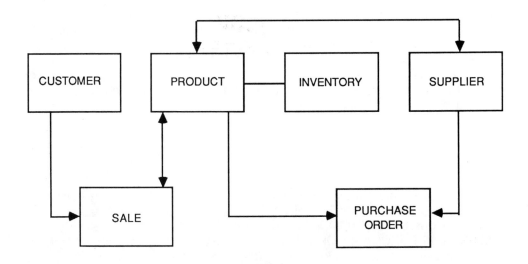

One of the most useful things about entity-relationship analysis is the knowledge that a many-to-many relationship can always be split into two one-to-many relationships by discovering the "intersection entity." Take, for example, the many-to-many relationship between products and sales:

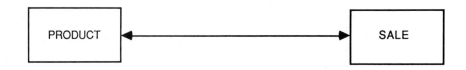

This can be thought of as being made up of two one-to-many relationships like the diagram on the next page:

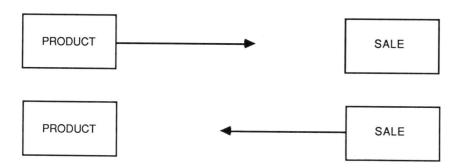

We put an "intersection" entity in between, with the "many" ends of the relationships ending on it:

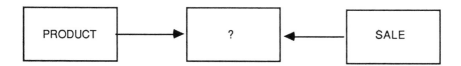

We then ask ourselves, "What is it that a single product may be associated with many of, and a single sale may be associated with many of, which expresses the relationship between products and sales?"

The answer, of course, is a sale item or sale item-line, the instance of one particular product being sold as part of a potentially multi-product sale:

Taking a similar approach to the many-to-many relationship between products and suppliers, we can discover another entity, the "PRODUCT_SOURCE," which expresses the fact that any one supplier will supply any one product at a given price and within a given quoted delivery time.

For each one-to-one relationship, we ask ourselves whether the two entities are truly separate, or can in fact be combined. In the case of products and inventories there would seem to be little case for having a separate table describing inventory.

So, putting all these considerations together, we would end up with a "resolved" entity-relationship diagram looking like this:

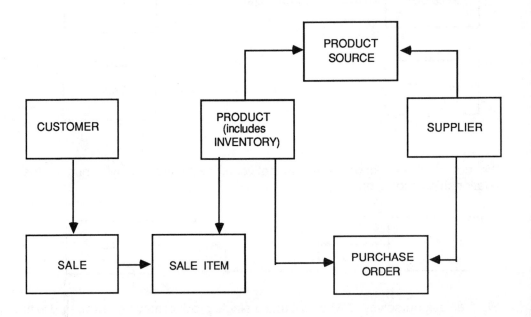

Entity-relationship analysis is a valuable way of getting insights into the overall structure of the data represented by the system. In some methodologies, such as Information Engineering, it is the principal analytical tool; in others it is used in conjunction with data flow analysis.

2.2 What is an entity? What is a relationship?

Entities are usually objects or events; for example, customers, suppliers, parts, products, people. Objects endure over time. Events occur at a specific moment. An object may have two or more events associated with it (the start and finish of a project; the hiring and termination of an employee). An event may represent an association between two or more objects (a customer ordering a product, an employee working on a project).

Something which does not involve at least two data elements to describe it is probably not an entity, but an attribute of something else or just a data element on its own. For example, while, on a strict definition, HIRE DATE could be considered to be an entity, it consists of only one data element, presumably describing an employee, and so would not be a very meaningful entity. The color "red" is not an entity; it could be a value of an attribute of an entity.

If an entity is something with multiple attributes, what is a relationship? Can relationships have attributes? If a relationship has attributes, how is it then different from an entity? Some analysts make a distinction, others do not. Some entities can be said to describe relationships. For example, on the page opposite, PRODUCT SOURCE could be said to hold information defining the "offers to sell" relationship between PRODUCT and SUPPLIER. Likewise, the PURCHASE ORDER entity could be said to hold information about the "is bought from" relationship between PRODUCT and SUPPLIER.

As well as these "information-bearing" relationship entities, we can identify non-information-bearing entities that describe relationships. Suppose we have an entity PROJECT with a key of PROJECT_ID. If we want to know who is assigned to what project, we could set up a table called, say, PROJECT ASSIGNMENT, that just lists a PERSON-ID and pairs it with a PROJECT_ID.

PROJECT	PROJECT ASSIGNMENT		PERSON
A274	A274	1001	1001
B397	A274	2002	2002
C49	B397	2002	
	C49	1001	
	C49	2002	

One person may work on many projects; one project may have many people assigned to it. PERSON and PROJECT thus have a many-to-many relationship. PROJECT ASSIGNMENT is the intersection entity that describes the relationship and only the relationship. It has no attributes, other than the two which are the keys to the basic entities; thus it is a non-information-bearing relationship-describing entity.

2.3   Describing relationships

We look at each pair of entities that we have identified, and ask what relationships, if any, must be recognized between them. The diagram shows the three types of possible relationships (one-to-one, one-to-many, and many-to-many).   Usually, as shown in the diagram, the description of the relationship is written along the line which joins the two entities. The arrowhead symbol is known as the "degree marker," or "cardinality indicator."

1:1

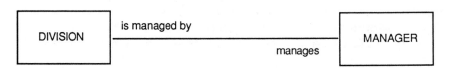

"Each Division is managed by one, and only one, Manager."
"Each Manager manages one, and only one, Division."

1:Many

"Each Sale involves one or more Sale Items."
"Each Sale Item is part of only one Sale."

Many:Many

"Each Supplier supplies one or more Products."
"Each Product is supplied by one or more Suppliers."

So the relationship between two entities on this type of diagram can be expressed in two sentences, each of which is the converse of the other, and each of which has the general form:

> "Each   *entity-name*
> *relationship-description-near-entity*
> *degree-marker-other-end*
> *other-entity"*

Sometimes there is more than one relationship between two entities.   For instance, PRODUCT and SUPPLIER may be associated both by "SUPPLIER offers PRODUCT" and "PRODUCT is bought from SUPPLIER," as shown here:

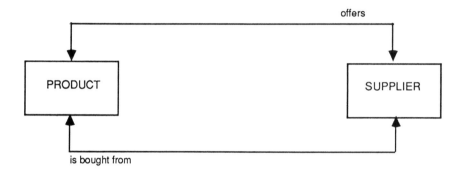

Optional relationship

Sometimes two entities may be related, but not in all instances.   Take EMPLOYEES and PROJECTS; an employee may be assigned to a project, or several projects, or none, while a project may be authorized, but not have anyone assigned to it yet.   This is shown as:

The open small circle means "a minimum of zero."

It's important to define whether relationships are optional or mandatory, especially when specifying a system in which the software is to enforce *referential integrity*; that is, to make sure that nothing is inserted into, or deleted from, the database which would make nonsense of some other entry.

For instance, in the 1:Many relationship between SALE and SALE ITEM above, it is clearly wrong to have one without the other: a SALE with no SALE ITEMs belonging to it is meaningless, a childless parent, while a SALE ITEM with no corresponding SALE is an orphan. Ideally, the database management system should not allow such a situation to arise. The filled-in circle shows that each SALE ITEM must be associated with a SALE, and vice versa.

Relationship to other occurrences of same entity

In some circumstances, an entity can be related to itself.

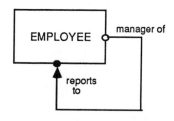

This diagram is to be read as:

"An employee may be manager of one or more other employe
"An employee always reports to another employee."

Either/or

Sometimes, it is necessary to show alternate possible relationships.   This is done by connecting the relationship lines to the same point:

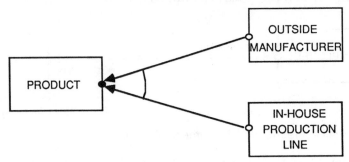

This diagram may be read as:

"A product must be associated either with one outside manufacturer or with one in-house production line. An outside manufacturer may supply many products. An in-house production line may supply many products."

2.4   Sub-types and super-types of entities

One frequently finds that several entities discovered during entity-relationship analysis are really different forms of the same entity.   Employees may be paid hourly, daily or monthly, may or may not be on commission, and may or may not be eligible for overtime.   But they are all people of interest to the system, with various classifications.   It's important to recognize the similarities of entities where they exist.   On an ERD, these similarities may be shown by drawing boxes within boxes, as shown below:

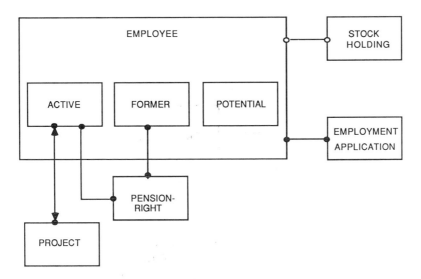

This diagram is to be read as saying that there are three sub-types of employees: active employees, former employees, and potential employees. Only active employees are associated with projects.   Any one active employee may be assigned to many projects.   Any one project may have many active employees assigned to it.

Each active and former employee is associated with a pension right.   Each pension right is associated with either an active employee or a former employee.

Potential employees (job applicants) have no pension rights (yet).

Every employee is associated with one employment application as the single line between the entity "EMPLOYMENT APPLICATION" and the super-type box "EMPLOYEE" shows.   Any one employee may be associated with a stockholding in the corporation.

Some CASE products show sub-types in an Entity Type Hierarchy Diagram like this:

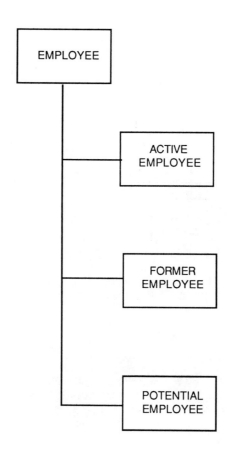

2.5   Other notations for ERDs

Chen notation

Peter Chen (Ref 2-1) recognizes a relationship between two entities as a separate construction on the diagram represented by a diamond.

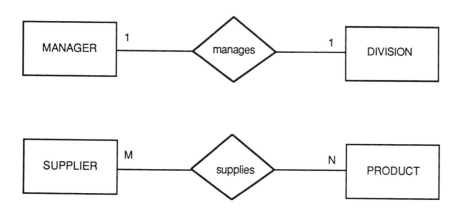

The "cardinality" of the association (whether it is 1:1, 1:Many, or Many:Many) is marked on the connecting lines.

Ross notation

Ronald Ross (Ref 2-2) also uses a diamond to represent a relationship or association, but uses single- or double-headed arrows to signify "1" or "Many."

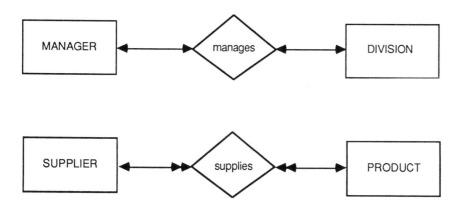

Ross also recognizes different types of entities, notably kernel entities, which can exist alone (such as customers or products), and characteristic entities (sometimes called dependent entities), which cannot exist without some kernel entity (such as customer accounts or employee assignments). Ross places a *c* in a small box in the upper-left corner of a characteristic entity block, like this:

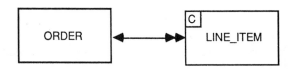

LBMS notation

Learmonth and Burchett Management Systems (LBMS), the vendors of the CASE product AUTOMATE-PLUS, recognize only one-to-many relationships in ERDs (which they call Logical Data Structures, or LDSs). Wherever a many:many relationship is found, they require that it should be documented via an intersection entity. So:

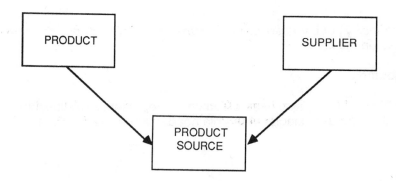

represents a many:many relationship between PRODUCT and SUPPLIER. (In an LDS, the single arrowhead means "many", and no arrowhead means "1".) An optional relationship is shown:

Ref 2-1 Chen, P. P. *Entity-Relationship Approach to Systems Analysis and Design.* Amsterdam: North Holland, 1980

Ref 2-2 Ross, R. G. *Entity Modeling: Techniques and Application.* Boston, MA: Database Research Group, 1987

Chapter 3

Graphical logical modelling: other techniques

3.1   Entity-life-history diagrams (ELHs)

The ELH is a technique supported by LBMS in their CASE product AUTOMATE-PLUS; it is a way of picturing the detailed logic of transactions which update the database, and it helps ensure that all error conditions are considered and provided for.

An ELH uses four symbols:

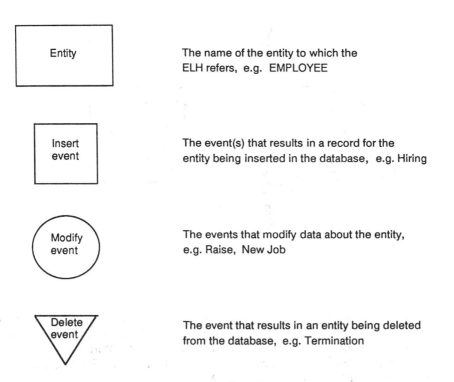

Entity	The name of the entity to which the ELH refers, e.g. EMPLOYEE
Insert event	The event(s) that results in a record for the entity being inserted in the database, e.g. Hiring
Modify event	The events that modify data about the entity, e.g. Raise, New Job
Delete event	The event that results in an entity being deleted from the database, e.g. Termination

Repetition of an event is shown with *, and clusters of events may be repeated.

Thus this ELH:

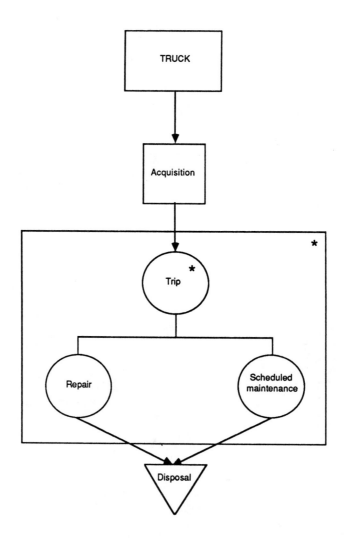

shows that each instance of entity TRUCK is initially acquired, which results in a record being inserted in the database, and then goes through multiple groups of multiple trips, followed by a repair or a scheduled maintenance, each of which updates the database, finally leading to an event of disposal (sale or scrapping), which causes the record to be deleted.

3.2   Decomposition diagrams

Many aspects of systems work involve hierarchies.   The parts of an organization, the reporting structures of managers, the breakdown of functions into smaller and smaller sub-functions, the breakdown of a document into chapters and sections, all can be documented as tree-structures, either "root-at-top":

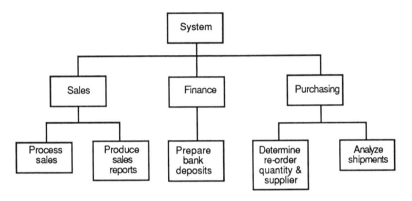

or "root-at-left":

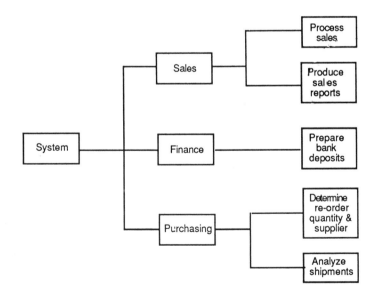

3.3   Matrices and affinity analysis

Many aspects of systems can be represented by matrices showing which
members of a set of entities or factors interact with which members of another
set.   To take a very simple example,   consider the DFD which we saw in
Chapter 1:

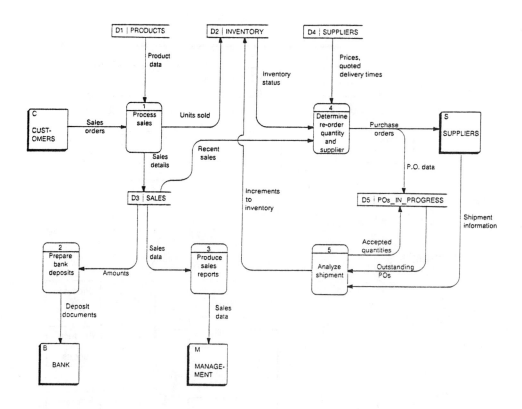

The processes interact with the data stores to create new records in them,
update them, or simply read them.   These interactions can be summed up in
the matrix on the next page.

Processes:

	1. Process sales	2. Prepare bank deposits	3. Produce sales reports	4. Determine reorder qty & supplier	5. Analyze shipment
Data stores:					
D1: PRODUCTS	R				
D2: INVENTORY	U			R	U
D3: SALES	C	R	R	R	
D4: SUPPLIERS				R	
D5: POS_IN_PROGRESS				C	RU

C = create
R = read
U = update
D = delete

This matrix is to be read as saying "Process 1 (Process Sales) **R**eads data store D1: PRODUCTS, **U**pdates D2: INVENTORY, and **C**reates records in D3: SALES" and so on. From the initial letters of the operations, this particular kind of data/process interaction matrix is known colloquially as a CRUD matrix.

Especially where large numbers of screens are being created by different analysts, it can be valuable to produce a matrix showing what data elements appear on what screens:

Screens:

	Screen 1	Screen 2	Screen 3	Screen 4	Screen 5
Data elements					
CUST_ID	E	D	E	D	D
CUST_ORGZN_NAME	D	E	D	D	E
LOCATION_CODE	D	E	D	D	E
CONTACT_FN	E	DM			DM
CONTACT_LN	E	DM			DM
CONTACT_PHONE	E	DM			DM
SMAN_CODE	D	DM		E	

E = entered
D = displayed
M = modified

On examination of this matrix, it appears that screen 5 uses all but one of the same data elements as Screen 2.   This suggests that, other things being equal, screen 2 could perhaps be re-used instead of Screen 5, and the system would be simplified.

Similarities like this may be hard to see even on simple matrices; obviously with 250 data elements and 100 screens, say, it would be almost impossible to pick out pairs of screens which had an affinity with one another, either because their data element usage was 100% the same, or because one used 95% of the same data elements (or 90%, or 85%, or whatever cut-off level you choose to set).

This is obviously a task that lends itself to machine processing by an affinity analysis program.   As an example of a CASE product which provides this facility, EXCELERATOR's analysis report "Equivalent Screen/Report Designs" lists pairs of Screen and/or Report designs (stored in the Repository) which use exactly the same data elements.   Its companion report, "Subset Screen/Report Designs," lists pairs where the elements used in one design are a subset of the elements used in another.

Chapter 4

Building a meta-data/ process repository

4.1   What is a repository?

The diagrams considered in the previous three chapters show the major objects involved in system definition and design: data stores,   entities,   processes, inflows,   outflows.   But they don't show the detail.   An entity called CUSTOMERS may really stand for an assemblage of, say, 93 data elements, which will end up as a group of tables in a relational database.   A process named "Analyze shipment" may stand for 8 pages of Structured English which will be implemented by 317 lines of COBOL.

When you look inside a data store, or an entity, or a data flow, you find one or more data structures: groupings of data elements and/or smaller data structures.   If you can define the component data elements and specify how they are combined in any instance, you can define any data object.   When you look inside a process, you see either a number of more detailed processes or basic process logic (sequences of actions,   rules for taking decisions,   and repetitions).

The analyst/designer needs a place to store all of this detail in machine-readable form, so that it can be manipulated easily: this storage is referred to as a "repository" or "design database,"   sometimes as the "project encyclopedia" or the "data dictionary."

The minimum a repository must do is to support the storage of detail about data structures,   data elements,   and process logic,   cross-referenced to the graphical models.   The repository may also be used to store physical structures such as screen designs, report designs, and database definitions, as well as system documentation and project documentation.   It follows that a repository contains meta-data (data describing data) plus data describing processes and other objects.

The repository may be held on the disk of an individual workstation, or held centrally, with each person on the project being able to read the central copy, and update it in a controlled way.   Some CASE products control sharing of the repository by dividing it into "sub-projects."   If an analyst decides to update the repository of a sub-project, it is locked by setting a flag which prevents anyone else from changing that sub-project until the first analyst has completed the updates. In some cases, a message is displayed to anyone who accesses the sub-project, saying in effect: "Joe has started to update this; if you read it, be aware that, at this very moment, Joe may be changing what you are looking at."

Other CASE products control sharing by locking only one object (e.g. a process description) at a time.

4.2   Data structures

A data structure (also called a data group, user-view, group data-item, or data aggregate) is a grouping of two or more data elements or data structures. Take a typical sales order: it will have a date, a customer name, address, and phone number, and one or more items which are being ordered. Each item may have a product code, a description, a price, a quantity, and an item-cost (price multiplied by quantity). Some orders may have a separate bill-to address, so this is an optional component.

So, to document the data structure, we have to specify the components, and to specify whether they are always present or are optional, and whether they may be repeated.

For example, we could use indentation to show inclusion:

```
SALES_ORDER
     ORDER_DATE
     CUST_NAME
     CUST_ADDRESS
     [BILL_TO_ADDRESS]              [ ] means "optional"
     SALES_ORDER_ITEM * (1-20)     * means repetition
                                   (1-20) means with a minimum
                                   of 1 occurrence, and a
                                   maximum of 20.
```

Clearly, SALES_ORDER_ITEM is also itself a data structure, thus:

```
SALES_ORDER_ITEM
     PRODUCT_CODE
     PRODUCT_DESCRIPTION
     UNIT-PRICE
     QUANTITY_ORDERED
     ITEM_COST
```

For that matter, CUST_ADDRESS and BILL_TO_ADDRESS are also data structures. Ideally, we will have an organization standard as to the contents of an address, so we don't need to redefine STREET, MAILSTOP, and so on; we just extract the standard definitions from the corporate data dictionary. What about CUST_NAME? Is that a data element, or will we need to store FIRST_NAME, MIDDLE_INITIAL, and LAST_NAME separately? One of the key analytical tasks is to make sure that, for any particular system, data is stored with as fine a grain as may be necessary.

So we can draw an ERD to show the structure of a data structure:

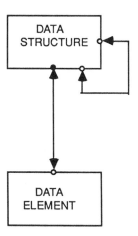

A data structure may contain one or more data structures; a given data structure may be contained in many other data structures.

It always contains two or more data elements; a given data element may be contained in many data structures.

Provided that all the data elements that make up all the component data structures are defined in the repository, we can completely specify a data structure by specifying what those components are, and how they are combined.

Key (identifier) elements

To define the contents of a data store or an entity, we want to be able to specify one or more data structures that will eventually be stored in the system's database. For such a data structure, one or more elements must be chosen to be the key, or identifier, in such a way that once you know the value of the key, you can pick out one and only one record from the database.

A key must be unique now and always, and once assigned, it should never change. Further, it must never have a missing or null value, because if it does, it may not be unique and certainly cannot be used as a cross-reference pointer from one data structure to another.

If a key cannot be found from the data elements which "naturally" describe each entity, then a unique identifier (such as EMPLOYEE_NO) must be created. This is a "dataless" or "arbitrary" key, assigned perhaps by the system incrementing a number for each new employee, which is stored *only* to provide a unique key.

Embedded structures

Particularly where keys have been inherited from older manual systems, one should watch out for the possibility that different parts of the key have special meanings. For instance, every book is assigned a unique ten-digit International Standard Book Number (ISBN), which has the format:

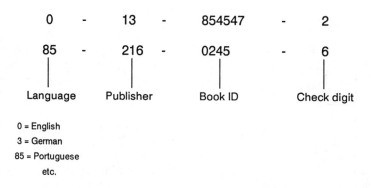

It may be desirable for the fields embedded in a common structure like this to be stored as separate data elements, so that one could, for example, sort all the books in a table by publisher's code.

4.3 Data element naming and description

Each data element should have a unique name, which should be as meaningful as possible without being inconveniently long. Especially if the nature of the data is not evident from the name, it is very convenient, during analysis, to have a description of each data element which fully explains the nature of the data itself. This description should be stored in the Repository.

Many approaches and conventions have been proposed for data naming. One workable approach is for the description of the data element to be in the form *"noun + of/which is + qualifier"* and for the name normally to be in the form *"qualifier + noun."*

Thus, a data element which would be described as "the quantity of a product which is the total on-order at any given time" or some such, would be given the name "ON_ORDER_QUANTITY."

A data element which would be described as "the date of actual shipment of a consignment from our premises" would be given the name, "ACTUAL_SHIPPING_DATE."

Description	Name	Abbreviated name
noun + of/which is + qualifier ...	qualifier + noun	
Quantity of a product which is on-order	ON_ORDER_ QUANTITY	ON_ORD_QTY
Date of actual shipment	ACTUAL_SHIPPING_ DATE	ACT_SHPG_DTE

One reason for adopting this format of the physical name is that, often, report generators use the physical element name as the heading of a column on a report and truncate the name to the default width of the column. The "qualifier + noun" format preserves the most meaning in such a circumstance, as the two examples below will show:

Data name	Truncated to six characters
QUANTITY_ON_ORDER	QUANTI
QUANTITY_IN_STOCK	QUANTI
ON_ORDER_QUANTITY	ON_ORD
IN_STOCK_QUANTITY	IN_STO

Partly for this reason, and also to save keystrokes, it's usually a good idea to have a set of minimum standard abbreviations for data names. A suggested list is given here; of course, many installations have their own list. Ideally, this list is on-line in a CASE package so that abbreviations can be automatically assigned.

ACTUAL	ACT
ADDRESS	ADDR
AMOUNT	AMT
AREA	AREA
BALANCE	BAL
BILLING	BLLG
CODE	CODE
CREDIT	CR
CURRENT	CURR
CUSTOMER	CUS
DATE	DTE
DEBIT	DR
DELIVERY	DELY
FIRST NAME	FN
IDENTIFIER	ID
INVENTORY	INVY
INVOICE	INVC
LAST NAME	LN
MIDDLE INITIAL	MI
MONTH	MTH
MONTH TO DATE	MTHTD
MONTHLY	MTHLY
NUMBER	NO
ORDER	ORD
OUTSTANDING	OS
PAYMENT	PAYT
PERSON	PER
PHONE	PHONE
PREVIOUS	PREV
PRODUCT	PROD
PROJECT	PROJ
PROJECTED	PROJD
PURCHASE	PUR
QUANTITY	QTY
QUARTER	QR
QUARTER TO DATE	QRTD
REGION	REGN
SALARY	SALRY
SALE	SALE
SALESMAN	SMAN
SHIPPING	SHPG
STATE	ST
STOCK	STK
STREET	STREET
SUPPLIER	SUP
UNITS	UTS
WEEKLY	WKLY
YEAR	YR
YEAR TO DATE	YRTD

Synonyms or aliases

In many cases, one finds that different names are used for the same entity in different parts of an organization. The terms "employee," "member of staff," "MOS," "personnel-cost-line-item," might be used in different systems departments to mean a person who works for the organization. These are synonyms; multiple names meaning the same underlying thing.

While it's better that synonyms should be avoided, they can be coped with by choosing one name to be the principal name and describing the others as the synonym or alias for that principal name.

Name   **Thing**

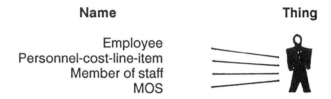

Employee
Personnel-cost-line-item
Member of staff
MOS

Homonyms

The converse situation exists when a given term can mean more than one thing or entity. A classic example is that of a projected delivery date. This seems a simple enough concept; the only problem with it is, where exactly is the delivery projected to take place? When the ship arrives in the harbor? When the goods are on the dock? When the goods are in the customs shed? When the goods have been cleared with customs? When the goods are actually delivered to our factory?

Name	**Thing**
Projected delivery date	Date that ship arrives in harbor
	Date that goods are released from customs
	Date that goods are in ready-use store

Take, again, the innocent-looking term "PRICE." Does this mean selling price, cost price, bulk price, or discounted price?

Such "homonyms" (where one word means more than one thing) are often hard to spot, because people in different departments can use the same terms (like "projected delivery date") among their own limited working group without any ambiguity.

In the Traffic Department, "projected delivery date" might mean the day the ship arrives in the harbor; in the Customs Brokering Department it might mean the day the goods are released from customs; in Production Control it might mean the day the goods are available, unpacked and checked, in the ready-use store. Within each small group no problem arises, because the term means only one thing: it's only when the analyst tries to create a system which crosses departmental boundaries that problems may arise unless the different meanings of the homonym are detected and dealt with.

The important issue is whether it will be completely clear, from the context in which the homonym is used, which of the various possible meanings it is to have. If it's not completely clear from the context, then each separate thing must be given a different name.

Naming the element after its domain

The domain of a data element is the set of all eligible values for that element. Thus the domain of a date might be any valid date later than January 1st, 1900. The domain of a temperature might be any value from − 273° to 5000°. If you know that a data element has a certain domain, you know the basic editing criteria for acceptable values (though not the rules for comparing one data element with another, such as that the hiring date must be earlier than the firing date). For this reason every domain should have a standard name, and where a data element belongs to a shared domain, its name should contain that domain's name, qualified if necessary.

So all dates should end in _DTE, and all salaries should end in _SALRY (not some _SAL and others _SALARY). Where no possibility of a homonym arises, the domain name alone can be used. Thus, in the CUSTOMER table, ZIP (the domain name) can be used unqualified; likewise in the EMPLOYEE table and in the SUPPLIERS table. No possibility of confusion exists.

Attributes of the domain and attributes of the data element

The name and one-sentence description of a data element are the basic facts about it, but for analysis to be complete, several other attributes of each data element need to be defined. Some of these attributes will be shared by every data element that belongs to a given domain; some attributes belong to only one particular data element.

Attributes shared by all data elements in a domain include:

1. **Data-type,** meaning whether numeric or string, plus length and format, if any. The exact data-types that data elements may be given vary from DBMS to DBMS. Some allow numeric domains to be integer, small integer, decimal, or floating-point, and allow string domains to contain any character, or only letters, and to be a normal length (for example, up to 255 characters long) or to be very long (for example, up to 4,096 characters long). Some DBMSs support a DATE data-type.

2. **Domain-type,** meaning whether the eligible values are defined by being on a list (a discrete domain, such as state-code) or by satisfying some rule (a continuous domain, such as salary or temperature). For a discrete domain, the eligible values need to be listed in a convenient table, together with the meaning of each value (since usually the meanings are used in the system). For a continuous domain, the defining rule has to be specified, giving the highest and lowest acceptable values where relevant.

3. One or more **examples of an eligible value** may be worth documenting. Rather than ask the users to specify the length of a field, it may be easier to ask for the largest/longest example the user can imagine. Could anyone have a salary over $1 million? What's the longest first name we should handle?

So a discrete domain might be defined as follows:

Domain name:	CITIZEN_STATUS
Data-type:	ALPHA length 1
Discrete or Continuous:	Discrete
Table of values/meanings:	CITIZEN_STATUS_MEANINGS
Contents:	Value Meaning

C	*US Citizen by birth*
N	*US Citizen by naturalization*
R	*Permanent resident with green card*
A	*Illegal alien, eligible for amnesty*
I	*Illegal alien, not eligible for amnesty*
V	*Visitor or other non-resident alien*

A continuous domain might be defined as:

Domain name:	PERSON_WEIGHT
Data-type:	INTEGER length 3
Discrete or continuous:	Continuous
High limit:	500
Low limit:	80
Other parts of defining rule:	Weight in pounds wearing underwear only, rounded to nearest pound

Attributes which are specific to a given data element (once you know its domain) are:

1.   The name of *this* data element. For instance, there might be several elements called APPLICANT_CITIZEN_STATUS, STOCKHOLDER_ CITIZEN_STATUS, CUSTOMER_CONTACT_CITIZEN_STATUS, and so on, all of which share the domain CITIZEN_STATUS.

2.   The description of *this* data element. Each data element above will have a slightly different description, though all share the same domain.

3.   Whether the data element is captured from outside the system, originated within the system, or derivable from other data elements. A captured data element must appear in some input dialogue; an originated data element (for example, a transaction identifier which is incremented by the system) must have the originating method specified; a derivable data element such as ITEM_TOTAL (derived from QTY * UNIT_PRICE) must have its derivation rule specified.

4.   The ownership of the data element, meaning the person or business unit responsible for its correctness, who has the final authority over whether the data element has been inserted or updated correctly.

So to summarize, the element-specific attributes of a data element are:

      Name
      Description
      Synonyms
      Source: Captured, Originated, or Derived
      If derived, from what other data elements and by what rule.
      Ownership

The domain-specific attributes are:

      Example
      Data-type   1.   inherent logical e.g. integer length 3
                     2.   as physically stored e.g. packed

      Domain type: Discrete or Continuous

            If discrete, table of values/meanings.
            If continuous, allowable range and/or other editing rules.

            Other validity rules, e.g. credit limit cannot be greater than $10,000 if customer is out-of-state, but can be up to $50,000 if in-state.

4.4 Process description

As we noted in Chapter 1, processes may be exploded into detailed DFDs which themselves contain processes. Depending on the approach you are taking, though, sooner or later you will end up with "primitive" processes which are to be described, rather than broken down further.

Each process will have a name (which should begin with a verb) and a reference number on the particular DFD in which it is used.

It will have at least one input data flow (carrying at least one data structure) and at least one output data flow, so by cross-reference a CASE product can work out the data elements coming into the process and going out of the process.

While not essential, it is convenient to have a short description of the process which summarizes its function, e.g.

> "Handles information about shipments received from suppliers, comparing quantities received with those on order, holding overshipments for the Buying Manager's disposal decision. Also produces Breakage Report."

The full logic of the process should be documented with Structured English, preferably in an Action Diagram like this:

```
 __
|    SHIPMENT PROCESSING
|      Enter first few letters of supplier name (or code, if known)
|
|    |== For each product in the shipment
|    |
|    |      Enter product name or key word
|    |      Retrieve outstanding POs for that product
|    |      Enter unbroken and broken items
|    |
|    |       __
|    |      |   IF unbroken items LE quantity outstanding on POs
|    |      |    __
|    |      |   |   IF more than 1 outstanding PO
|    |      |   |      Decide which PO(s) to apply items to
|    |      |   |
|    |      |   |   ELSE (only 1 PO)
|    |      |   |__    Apply whole accepted quantity
.    .    .
.    .    .
etc.              For details of action diagramming, see Chapter 6.
```

Volume and triggering events

For each process, the analyst should be able to answer the questions "How often does this happen?" and "When or under what circumstances does it happen?" Volume or frequency may be given as a likely minimum or maximum per day, week, month, etc., or as a starting number with an expected growth rate up to the maximum that the system should be designed to handle.

Processes are usually triggered either by input (such as a customer inquiring about a price) or by a time (such as an end-of-day report) or by management demand (such as an ad hoc inventory breakdown request).

So putting all the attributes of a process together, we have:

DFD or other diagram on which it appears, plus reference number on that diagram

Process name

Short description

Inflows and outflows

Volume/frequency

Triggering condition(s)/event(s)

Detailed logic

Chapter 5

Data analysis: normalization

5.1 Simplifying data structures through normalization

In Chapter 4 we discussed data structures without worrying whether they were simple or complex. The technique of "normalization" provides a systematic way of boiling data structures down to their simplest possible forms. This is an important step in database design, particularly for relational DBMSs.

In database discussions the word "relation" means a table of data; it follows that a relational database is one made up of a group of linked tables.

The term "relation" derives from the study of data made by E. F. (Ted) Codd and others, then at IBM, trying to think out a theoretically sound way of describing data that would lead to the design of flexible, changeable data structures (Ref 5-1). In thinking about data, Codd found the mathematics of sets to be helpful. A mathematical set may be thought of as a group of objects with an associated defining rule or list that enables you to tell whether a given object is in the set or not. Thus, the set of all even numbers is a subset of the set of all numbers, with the defining rule that each member is exactly divisible by 2. The set of white rabbits is a subset of the set of all rabbits, with the defining property that the animal has white fur all over, and so on.

Any given data value may be thought of as a member of the set of all possible values for that data element; thus the state-code "NY" is a member of the set of all valid state-codes. As we noted earlier, the set of all eligible values for a data element is called its "domain," usually defined either by a list or by upper and lower bounds. The domain of SALARY might be any number with two decimal places between 4999.99 and 100000.00; the domain of AIRPORT_CODE is a list of three-letter groups like JFK, LAX and so on.

If you have several domains defined, it is possible to make another set by taking a value from domain 1, a value from domain 2, and so on. By analogy with words like "quintuple" and "octuple," such a set is called a "tuple." A tuple with values from each of two domains (for example, CA, California) is a 2-tuple, from three domains a 3-tuple, and so on. If you have a set of 2-tuples such that for every member of the domain STATE_CODE there was a corresponding member of the domain STATE_NAME, you would have a table of state-code meanings. For this set of tuples to be useful, you would need to know what each domain signified (translation: the table would have to have headings). So we come to the formal definition of a relation: "A set of domain-names plus a set of tuples, where each tuple consists of a set of name-value pairs, one pair for each domain, where the value is drawn from the domain of that name."

The STATE_CODE/STATE_NAME relation can be written out:

```
( STATE CODE : CA       )   ( STATE NAME : California )
( STATE CODE : FL       )   ( STATE NAME : Florida    )
( STATE CODE : AK       )   ( STATE NAME : Alaska     )
.
.
```

Note that there is nothing in this definition about the sequence of the tuples, and that's something to bear in mind when we show the relation in the more familiar form of a table:

```
STATE CODE STATE NAME              STATE NAME STATE CODE
---------- ----------   or we      ---------- ----------
CA         California   could      Florida    FL
FL         Florida      show it    New Jersey NJ
AK         Alaska       as:        California CA
NJ         New Jersey              Alaska     AK
.
.
```

From the relational point of view, these tables are identical; the sequence from left to right, or from top to bottom, means nothing and holds no information about the data. So when we say that a relation is a table, it is a table with this special nature. Part of the flexibility of a relational database comes from this property; no information is "hidden" in the physical layout of the database.

To summarize this terminology:

Set theory	Relational database	Conventional DP
Relation	Table	File
Domain	All the possible values a column can have	All the possible values a field can have
Tuple	Row	Record

In a mathematical set, no duplicates of any object are allowed. Since a relation is a set of tuples, in theory no row in a relation can be a duplicate of any other row. (In practice, SQL allows you to have duplicate rows in a table, though there are ways of eliminating them if you want to.) As we noted in the previous section, if a column or concatenation of columns cannot be found to uniquely identify each row, then a special key column must be invented.

Normalization of relations (simplification of tables)

Some tables are easier to change than others. Considerable attention has been given to tests for ease of changeability; five types of tables, called in the jargon "normalized forms," have been identified.

First normal form (1NF)

Any table that has only one value per cell, or row/column intersection, is in 1NF. The table

```
    Part #        Depots at which stored
    ------        ----------------------
    T232          Chicago,  Denver,  Orlando
    H995          Denver,  Chicago
    .
    .
```

is not in any normal form; it is unnormalized.

However, the table

Part #	Depot	In-stock qty	Depot phone	Number of containers
T232	Chicago	467	312/222-9876	47
T232	Denver	319	313/675-9786	32
T232	Orlando	121	305/745-0934	13
H995	Denver	578	313/675-9786	58
H995	Chicago	227	312/222-9876	23
.				
.				

is in first normal form.

Second normal form (2NF)

To test whether a table is in second normal form, we ask:

1.   What is the key to this relation?   If the key is concatenated (more than one column), we then also ask:

2.   Are there any non-key columns that depend on only part of the key?

For the table above, what is the key? Clearly, "Part #" alone is not enough to uniquely identify a given row; we need to concatenate "Depot" with "Part #" to get a unique key.

Since the key is concatenated, we will also ask the second question.

Does "In stock qty" depend on only part of the key?   No; you have to know both the Part # and the Depot.

Does "Depot phone" depend on only part of the key?   Yes; if you know the Depot, you know its phone, without caring about the Part #.   The table above is therefore not in second normal form, since it does not pass the test:

A first normal form table is also in second normal form if every non-key column depends on the whole of the key.

What is wrong with having a table in first normal form?

1.   The database will take up more room on disk than it need do, since the phone number is repeated for every part stored in the same depot.

2.   If a depot changes its phone number, the change must be made to every row for a part in that depot.

3.   If anything goes wrong with the updating process, a depot may appear to have different phone numbers depending on which row is retrieved later on; the integrity of the database will be lost.

4.   If the whole row for a part is deleted when the part is not stored in a given depot, there may be nowhere in the database to store the phone number of a depot, just because it happens to be empty for the time being.

To avoid these disadvantages, the table above must be split into two tables:

PART_STORAGE

Part #	Depot	In-stock qty	Number of containers
T232	Chicago	467	47
T232	Denver	319	32
T232	Orlando	121	13
H995	Denver	578	58
H995	Chicago	227	23
.			
.			
.			

DEPOT_DATA

Depot	Depot phone
Chicago	312/222-9876
Denver	313/675-9786
Orlando	305/745-0934
.	
.	
.	

Both of these tables are in 2NF. The top table, PART_STORAGE, is in 2NF because both the non-key columns ("In-stock qty" and "Number of containers") are dependent on the concatenated key, the whole concatenated key, and nothing but the concatenated key. The second table, DEPOT_DATA, is automatically in 2NF because it does not have a concatenated key, and so the non-key column "Depot phone" must naturally be dependent on the whole of the single key column "Depot."

Looked at another way, the 1NF table is holding facts that describe two separate things: the storage of parts, and the depot in which they are stored. As a general rule, one table in a database should describe only one entity; it should contain facts about only one thing or class of things.

Third normal form (3NF)

To test whether a 2NF table is also in 3NF, we ask, "Are any of the non-key columns dependent on any other non-key columns?" PART_STORAGE has two non-key columns. If you know a value for "In-stock qty," do you then know the corresponding value for "Number of containers?" Well, maybe you do; the table shows that all parts are packed in containers of 10, so the number of containers can be derived from the quantity by dividing by 10 and rounding up to cover part-empty containers. So there is a dependency between the two non-key columns created by this "business rule," and PART_STORAGE is not in 3NF, though it can be made so by removing "Number of containers," saving space and possible loss of integrity. (If the business rule were different, and each individual container held a different number of parts, then the number of containers would be an independent fact, and PART_STORAGE would be in 3NF as it stands above.) The rule is:

A second normal form table is also in third normal form if no non-key column depends on any other non-key column.

Another common case met with in normalization arises with a table like:

```
EMPLOYEE_NO      DEPARTMENT      BUILDING
-----------      ----------      --------
26622            Sales           West block
41156            Accounts        Headquarters
33987            Research        North Lab
88644            Sales           West block
```

This table is in 1NF; it does not have a concatenated key since EMPLOYEE_NO uniquely identifies each row, so it is automatically also in 2NF. Is there a dependency between the non-key columns? Well, it depends. If it is the case that a department is housed in only one building, then if you know the department, you know the building, so the table is not in 3NF and should be split into:

```
EMPLOYEE_NO   DEPARTMENT     and     DEPARTMENT   BUILDING
```

If, on the other hand, employees work all over, wherever space can be found, then the building is a fact about an employee, not about a department, and the table above *is* in 3NF.

This brings up the issue of changeability of table design. What would happen if the business changed three months after the system was implemented, so that whereas each department used to be in a given building, employees now work all over? The two-table design will now not hold the necessary facts, and the database will have to be restructured, back to the one-table design.

Consequently, if the designer suspects that the present business situation might change, it would be prudent to implement the one-table design, which is more changeable, even though it is initially in 2NF and involves redundant information (at present).

Note how simplification of data requires knowledge of the business, of the "business rules" which set up relationships between data elements, and of possible changes in those business rules.

Fourth normal form (4NF)

As a general rule, 3NF tables are easy to understand, easy to update, and easy to retrieve data from. Occasionally, though, a problem arises if a given non-key column can have multiple values for a given key value. Consider:


```
FACULTY_MEMBER        COURSE_TAUGHT        DEGREE
--------------        -------------        ------
Poindexter            Biology 101          AB
Poindexter            Statistics 703       BS
Poindexter                                 MA
Poindexter                                 PhD
Farthingale           Statistics 703       AB
Farthingale           Poetry 666
Farthingale           Relativity 900
```


What is the key for this table? FACULTY_MEMBER is not a unique identifier; neither is the concatenation of FACULTY_MEMBER and COURSE_TAUGHT, as the third and fourth rows show; neither is the concatenation of FACULTY_MEMBER and DEGREE. We are forced to conclude that the key is the concatenation of all three columns. Since there are no non-key columns, the table must be in 2NF and in 3NF, passing both tests. It still has a problem, though. If Poindexter is assigned three more classes, how will the table be updated? Will three more rows be inserted with null DEGREEs, or will existing null slots be filled up and then another row inserted, or what? This table fails the test for 4NF:

> *A third normal form table is also in fourth normal form if it does not contain more than one multi-valued fact about the entity described by the table.*

The table is trying to hold two multi-valued facts: the various courses taught and the degrees held. Even though it is in 3NF, the fact that it holds more than one multi-valued fact makes it hard to update.

The table needs to be split into two tables, both of which are now in 4NF.

```
FACULTY_MEMBER COURSE_TAUGHT
-------------- -------------
Poindexter     Biology 101
Poindexter     Statistics 703
Farthingale    Statistics 703
Farthingale    Poetry 666
Farthingale    Relativity 900
```

```
FACULTY_MEMBER DEGREE
-------------- ------
Poindexter     AB
Poindexter     BS
Poindexter     MA
Poindexter     PhD
Farthingale    AB
```

If Poindexter now is given three more classes, or Farthingale gets her PhD, the update procedure is quite clear and simple.

Fifth normal form (5NF)

In some even rarer instances, it may be simpler to split a 4NF relation up into two or more tables.

> *A fourth normal form relation is in fifth normal form when its information content cannot be reconstructed from several smaller relations not having the same key.*

For a discussion of 5NF, see Reference 5-2.

5.2   Code-interpretation tables

As you can see from the previous section, the process of normalization results in the production of numerous tables.   A good proportion of the tables that result, however, have only two columns: a code of some kind, and the meanings to be attached to this code.

Consider the table:

```
FLT_NO DEPART FROM_CODE FROM_AIRPORT   TO_CODE    TO_AIRPORT
------ ------ --------- -------------- ---------- ----------
996    1230   SFO       San Francisco JFK        NY-Kennedy
 .
 .
 .
```

This cannot be in third normal form because there is a dependency between non-key fields: If you know a code, you know the airport name.   The table should be broken into two:

ROUTINGS

```
        FLT_NO DEPART FROM_CODE TO_CODE
        ------ ------ --------- --------
        996    1230   SFO       JFK
         .
         .
         .
```

STATION_CODES

```
        CODE AIRPORT_NAME
        ---- -----------------
        DFW  Dallas-Fort Worth
        JFK  NY-Kennedy
        SFO  San Francisco
         .
         .
```

Two-column tables like STATION_CODES will be referred to as "code-interpretation" tables.   They typically hold data that is relatively stable (airport codes and state codes are very rarely changed, and a marital status of M will mean "MARRIED" for a long time to come).   A fully normalized data model typically has a sizable number of such code-interpretation tables.

5.3 Automated help with normalization

While no CASE product has yet been developed that enables you to feed in a data structure and get out a set of 3NF relations, some (for example, BACHMAN's DataAnalyst and LBMS's AUTOMATE-PLUS) offer interactive help with the process.

In general terms, a normalization dialog allows you to name a previously defined data structure (the subject). If the subject contains any repeating structures, the CASE tool will break the subject up into, perhaps, a header structure containing the elements that don't repeat and a separate detail structure. The tool will then ask you to identify the key for each structure, or to supply/invent a key if none exists.

Then, taking each subject substructure in turn, if the key is a concatenated one, the tool will ask you to point to any of the non-key fields that depend on only part of the key.

If there are any such fields, the tool will split the structure up again, and repeat the process. When you get down to a structure which has only one data element as the key (and so is automatically in 2NF), or one for which you say there is no partial key dependency, the CASE tool then will ask you whether there is a dependency between any of the non-key elements, and if so, what depends on what. The software then will remove the dependent element to another table.

Lastly, the software can look for data structures in the Repository that have identical keys and ask you if it makes sense to put them together into one single relation.

Note that in a dialog of this nature, the software is acting as your clerical assistant. You are making judgments about dependencies between elements, and the software is merely acting on the consequences of your decisions.

References

Ref 5-1 Codd, E. F. *A relational model of data for large shared data banks.* Communications of the ACM, June 1970.

Ref 5-2 Kent, W. *A simple guide to five normal forms in relational database theory.* Communications of the ACM, February 1983.

Chapter 6

Process design

6.1 Screen painting and prototyping

A large class of systems use what we shall refer to as fixed-layout text/data (FLTD) screens. On an FLTD screen, some text appears (perhaps a screen header), with prompts beside or above areas where data values are to be entered or displayed. Data values may be singular (one prompt, one value), or may be in multiple-line areas, with or without scrolling. The screen layout may be clarified by lines or boxes using graphic characters. A simple FLTD screen is shown here:

```
== Handy Hardware Inc., 10000 Broadway, Erewhon City ==  Sale no: 100001
Salesperson: AAA            Wednesday 10 Sep 86  11:14 am     Tax rate % : 5
- - - - - - - - - - - - - - - - - - - - - - - - - - - - - - - - - - - - -
Code  Item         Description      Price  Qty  $-cost     Tax   Item tot
H995  Bucket       24 quart         10.95    1   10.95    0.55     11.50
H134  Refuse bin   Pedal opening    13.25    2   26.50    1.33     27.83
T232  Wrench       Adjustable       13.95    3   41.85    2.09     43.94




                                                         -----   -------
                                      Sale totals:        3.97     83.27
- - - - - - - - - - - - - - - - - - - - - - - - - - - - - - - - - - - - -
How paid  (CAsh,AX,VI,MC): CA                      Cash tendered:   90.00
                                                 Amount of change:   6.73

=== Thank you for shopping at Handy;  for delivery call 212/245-8870 ===
```

An FLTD screen, of course, is to be distinguished from a line-by-line screen, such as that produced by a terminal session where the user responds to a prompt, perhaps by entering a command, and the system responds with one or more lines of output.

It also is to be distinguished from a pull-down menu and/or windowed screen, in which the appearance of the screen at any time during execution depends on the sequence in which pop-up windows have been selected.

Most screen-painters only create FLTD screens. Typically, you can move the cursor to a place where you want text to appear, key in the text, then move the cursor to the start of a data area, press a pre-set function key to indicate that you want a data value, and enter the name of the corresponding data element. If the screen-painter is integrated with the Repository, the length of the data-element is extracted, and a suitably sized data area is set up. If you want to adjust the layout, you place the cursor on the field or text-block to be moved, press a "Move" function key, and then point to the new place.

If the screen-painter is fully integrated with the Repository, and if the data-types and editing rules for each data element are defined in the Repository, then the CASE tool has all the information needed to generate a data entry prototype, where an error message is displayed if an invalid value is entered in any field.

Once data is entered, it can be stored in a prototype database and used to display prototype queries. Further logic needs to be added, of course, to display any kind of computation (such as multiplying Quantity by Unit-price).

6.2 Dialog planning diagrams

Where a dialog involves menus that lead to menus that, in turn, lead to more menus, it is convenient to have a picture of the structure.

6.2.1 Invocation dialog structure (IDS) diagrams

LBMS's AUTOMATE-PLUS supports a technique for showing which screen can invoke which other screen(s). An invocation dialog structure has two key symbols.

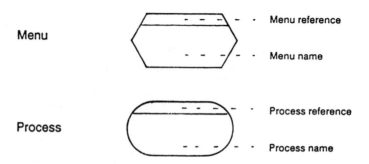

Thus this IDS:

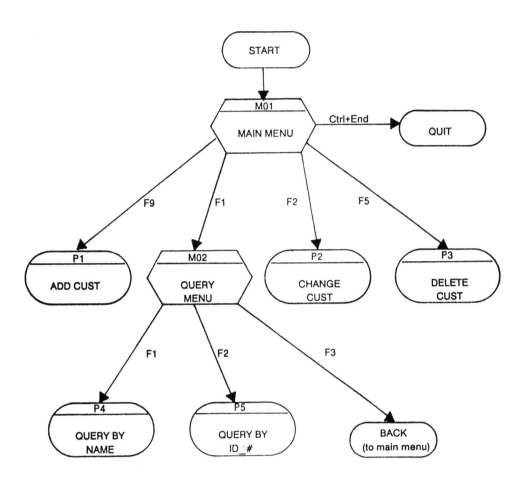

shows a (simplified) structure in which the operator can choose from the main menu (by pressing the appropriate function keys) to add a new customer, query the database, change an existing customer, or delete an existing customer.

If the operator presses F1 to query the database, a query menu is displayed with three choices, and so on.

6.2.2   Dialog flow diagrams

This is an alternative way of showing the possible transitions from menu to screen to screen:

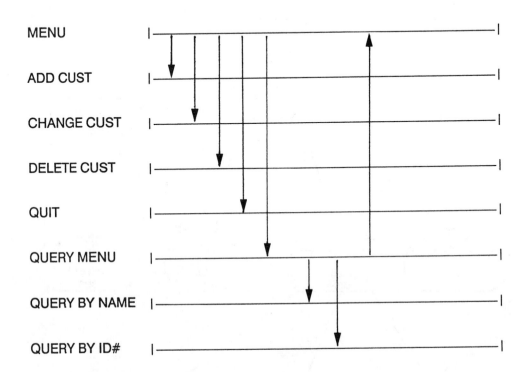

MENU

ADD CUST

CHANGE CUST

DELETE CUST

QUIT

QUERY MENU

QUERY BY NAME

QUERY BY ID#

6.2.3   Caller/operator/machine dialog scripts

No matter what the degree of division of labor, it is important (and tricky) to think clearly about multi-screen dialogs.   There are often three actors in the dialog: the operator, the system, and someone on the phone with whom the operator is having a conversation.   The dialog may branch depending on what the caller says and what the system says, and the branching structure itself needs to be planned and controlled.   There are two approaches to specifying dialogs: the multi-column script and the playscript.

Multi-column script

The next page shows a sample multi-column dialog display.

External event/ condition	Operator says/does	Operator enters	System displays	System action
START			Main menu	
IF caller says something like "I'm interested in [author]'s book on [subject], [title]		I for Inquiry/Order		GO TO Screen 1
ELSE IF				
Caller says:				
"I ordered a book and it hasn't come" **OR** "You sent me wrong/ damaged book"		E for Existing order		GO TO Screen 2
ELSE IF				
Caller says anything else		P for Problems		GO TO Screen 3

Screen 1: Inquiry/order   Invoked from: Main menu

(The screen layout may be inserted here or kept in a separate part of the document)

External event/ condition	Operator says/does	Operator enters	System displays	System action
		Whatever info caller gave		Retrieve books based on author name, and/or subject, and/or title keywords
IF no hit, or too many to read out				
	Ask caller for more info			
ELSE	Give caller price and delivery; ask for order			
IF caller does not want to order,				
	Thank for calling	Esc		GO TO START
ELSE	Ask for shipment details			
		▪ ▪ ▪		

In column 1, the external events and conditions that trigger the dialog are tabulated (including things the caller says), together with labels for the control flow and logical connectors, such as IF and ELSE.

In column 2, the operator's actions are tabulated, other than entering data into the system, which is in column 3.   Columns 4 and 5 tabulate the system's external and internal actions, respectively.

If there were no human dialog, the chart might need only columns 3, 4, and 5, which would correspond to the system's input, output, and processing, respectively.   If you want to concentrate only on the human dialog and/or manual procedures, they are shown in columns 1 and 2.

The multi-column script lends itself to being built up piecemeal, perhaps in a group workshop. Large pieces of paper are ruled with the five columns; each entry may be written on an adhesive label, so that it can easily be moved around as the dialog evolves.

Play script

The other representation of a dialog is the playscript, so called because it is similar to the text of a play, with the addition of a left-hand column to hold labels and logical connectors, as shown here:

Label/ logic	Player	Action
START	System	Displays main menu
IF	Caller	Says something like "I'm interested in [author]'s book on [subject], [title]..."
THEN	Operator System	Enters I for Inquiry/Order GO TO Screen 1
ELSE IF	Caller	Says "I ordered a book and it hasn't come" OR "You sent me wrong/damaged book"
THEN	Operator System	Says "Sorry, let me get your record" Enters E for Existing Order GO TO Screen 2
ELSE IF	Caller	Says anything else
THEN	Operator System	Enter P for Problems GO TO Screen 3
. . .		

This representation stresses the sequence of events, but it does not make it so easy to separate the two conversations.

Both the multi-column script and the playscript take up about the same amount of space. The playscript is somewhat easier to handle on a word processor.

Both examples present a three-way branch from the main menu. Clearly, the designer must be concerned with the control structure implied by the dialog. No endless loops should be created: Every path taken should eventually end up back at the START label.

In designing the control structure of a dialog, it is worth remembering the constructs of structured programming. Every procedure - not just every computer program - can be built out of combinations of three building blocks:

- a single-entry, single-exit sequence of operations

- a single-entry, single-exit loop or repetition structure

- an IF-THEN-ELSE decision structure.

Where several mutually exclusive conditions are being tested for (such as where a person may be under 16, between 16 and 21, between 21 and 65, or over 65), an IF-ELSE IF-ELSE IF ... decision structure is used (sometimes called a CHOOSE or CASE structure because it deals with different cases). A CASE structure is reducible to binary IF-THEN-ELSEs; it's just more meaningful when mutually exclusive cases are encountered.

If you are in doubt about the clarity of the control structure of a dialog, it is a good idea to step back from the detail and restructure the dialog using the structures above. The technique of action diagramming is a help in doing this.

6.3 Action Diagrams and Structured English

Structured English is a limited subset of English for describing procedures, consisting of:

- imperative sentences starting with action verbs (for example, "Multiply quantity by unit price")

- no undefined adjectives

- labels and/or logical connectors and/or conditions to show the structure

Some examples are given in the following pages; for more details, see Ref 6-1.

Sequence block

A single-entry single-exit block composed of a non-branching series of operations is shown like this:

```
|--[NAME]                                --|    [Input(s)]
|                                          |
|   Action A                               |
|                                          |
|   Action B                               |
|                                          |
|   Action C                               |
|--                                      --|    [Output(s)]
```

The start and end of the block is shown by the vertical bracket at the left. If the block is to be referred to by name, the name should be placed as shown. If you know the inputs and outputs for the block, you may optionally show them outside a vertical bracket at the right of the block.

For example, a block named "Compute hypotenuse of right triangle" may be shown like this:

```
|--Compute hypotenuse of right triangle--|    lengths of 2
|                                         |    shorter sides
|   Square length of Side 1               |
|   Square length of Side 2               |
|   Add squares together                  |
|   Take square root of sum               |
|                                       --|    length of
|--                                       |    hypotenuse
```

Loop block

A loop block is denoted by two = signs at the start. It may be given a name, but it must always have the condition that specifies when the loop should terminate.

This may be in the form "For all ...." or "DO WHILE some condition is true."

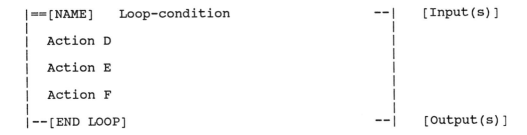

```
|==[NAME]    Loop-condition                    --|   [Input(s)]
|                                               |
|   Action D                                    |
|                                               |
|   Action E                                    |
|                                               |
|   Action F                                    |
|                                               |
|--[END LOOP]                                  --|   [Output(s)]
```

As with a sequence block, if the inputs and outputs for the loop are known, they may be listed at the right.

As an example:

```
|==IDENTIFY REORDER CANDIDATES.  For all products:
|
|   Retrieve quantity in stock now.
|
|   Compute average sales per day over last 7 days.
|
|   Compute how-many-days-stock-will-last.
|
|   Retrieve max(quoted-delivery-time) from supplier
|       quotations into longest-quoted-delivery time.
|
|   IF longest-quoted-delivery-time  LE
|       how-many-days-stock-will-last.
|
|       Insert product-details into reorder-candidate list.
|
|--END LOOP
```

Decision block

Decision blocks are of two kinds: the binary IF-ELSE structure, in which one of two possibilities must apply, and the CASE structure, in which several mutually exclusive possibilities are tested for, only one of which can apply.

The binary IF-ELSE is shown thus:

```
|--IF condition
|
|   Action P
|
|   Action Q
|
|--ELSE (not-condition)
|
|   Action R
|
|   Action S
|
|--[END IF]
```

It is good practice to spell out the situation that would cause the "ELSE" branch to be taken; that way the structured English is more readable.

The CASE structure is shown like this:

```
|--IF condition A
|
|--ELSE IF condition B
|
|--ELSE IF condition C
|
|--ELSE (none of the above)
```

(As mentioned earlier, the CASE structure can be reduced to binary IF-ELSEs in theory; in practice it makes more sense to display the alternatives as shown.)

You should always remember, and deal with, the possibility of the dangling ELSE at the end of the block; this covers the situation that will arise if none of the mutually exclusive conditions apply. For example:

```
|--IF person is under 21
|      Covered under policy of parent
|
|--ELSE IF person is 21 - 35 inclusive
|      Premium is $150 per $1,000
|
|--ELSE IF person is 36 - 65 inclusive
|      Premium is $100 per $1,000
|
|--ELSE (person is over 65)
|      Policy is not available
```

Abnormal exit

In some blocks, a condition may arise that makes continued normal processing impossible. Control needs to go directly to the exit of the block. Such a situation may be shown like this:

```
|--ROUTINE
|
|   Action A
|
|   Action B
|
|<-IF out-of-range   GO TO END ROUTINE
|
|   Action C
|
|   Action D
|
|--END ROUTINE
```

Note that a GO TO which moves control forward to an exit is not a violation of structured programming principles, because the block still has only one exit.

In practice, the various kinds of blocks are nested together. Consider the procedure that we began to lay out in the earlier dialog.

If the caller is interested in a certain book, the operator has to enter whatever information the caller provides: the title, if the caller knows it, and/or the author's name, and/or any words indicating the title or the subject. The system will then search for all books in the database that match those criteria. If nothing is retrieved, presumably the caller is asking about a book which either is so new that it is not in the database yet, or is out of print. The operator should enter whatever details the caller can provide, promise that the book buyer (who knows the field) will research the title and get back to him or her, and ask what other books the caller is interested in.

If the details of the book are retrieved, the operator should give the caller the price and delivery time (displayed on the screen), and if the caller wants to order, enter the quantity and enter how the caller wants the book(s) shipped (book rate, UPS, etc.). If the caller doesn't want to order this book, the operator should ask whether he's interested in any other book.

This procedure could be represented by an action diagram thus:

```
|==For each book customer is interested in
|
|   Enter title or author name or key word
|
|   Search for matching titles
|
|   |--IF no hit
|   |
|   |   Enter whatever information customer has
|   |   Promise you'll research the book and get back to him
|<-|--Go on to next book
|   |
|   |--ELSE (book details retrieved)
|   |
|   |   Quote customer price and delivery time
|   |
|   |   |--IF customer wants to order
|   |   |    Enter quantity and shipment method
|   |   |
|   |   |--ELSE (doesn't want this book)
|   |   |    Ask if he's interested in any other book
|   |   |--ENDIF
|   |
|   |--ENDIF
|
|--END LOOP
```

This structure might itself be nested within a more comprehensive structure covering the whole order processing dialog:

```
|--ORDER ROUTINE
|
|   Get customer phone number and enter
|
|   Retrieve cust record:display at bottom of screen if found
|
|   |==For each book customer is interested in
|   |
|   |   Enter title or author name or key word
|   |
|   |   Search for matching titles
|   |
|   |   |--IF no hit
|   |   |
|   |   |   Enter whatever information customer has
|   |   |   Promise you'll research the book and get back to him
|   <-|   --Go on to next book
|   |   |
|   |   |--ELSE (book details retrieved)
|   |   |
|   |   |   Quote customer price and delivery time
|   |   |
|   |   |   |--IF customer wants to order
|   |   |   |    Enter quantity and shipment method
|   |   |   |
|   |   |   |--ELSE (doesn't want this book)
|   |   |   |    Ask if he's interested in any other book
|   |   |   |--ENDIF
|   |   |
|   |   |--ENDIF
|   |
|   |--END LOOP
|
|   |--IF customer has ordered anything
|   |
|   |   Enter shipping address/confirm if already retrieved
|   |   Enter billing address if different
|   |
|   |--ELSE (just an inquiry)
|   |
|   |   |--IF cust wants to be on mailing list
|   |   |
|   |   |   Enter/confirm address
|   |   |
|   |   |--ELSE (no interest)
|   |   |
|   |   |   Delete if displayed
|   |   |
|   |   |--ENDIF
|   |
|   |--ENDIF
|
|   Thanks for calling
|-- END ROUTINE
```

Once the dialog is in this form, you can be confident that it has clean logic, with all logical possibilities considered, and without "spaghetti" control flows.   The action diagram can be used either as the basis for prototyping, or for code generation, or it can be converted to one of the dialog script formats, giving the operator detailed instructions as to what to say and do.

For more information on action diagrams, see Ref 6-2.

6.4   Structure charts

Consider this piece of pseudo-code:

```
PROCESS_A_TRANS
     DO SET_UP
     WHILE THERE ARE MORE TRANSACTIONS
          DO GET_A_TRANS  RETURNING RAW_TRANS
          DO VALIDATE_A_TRANS SENDING RAW_TRANS
                                RETURNING GOOD_OR_BAD
        IF GOOD_OR_BAD IS BAD
             DO REPAIR_A_TRANS   SENDING BAD_TRANS
                                 RETURNING OK_TRANS
        END IF
        DO PROCESS_GOOD_TRANS    SENDING OK_TRANS
                                 RETURNING RESULT
          DO WRITE_RESULT        SENDING RESULT
     END_LOOP
     DO CLOSE_DOWN
```

It represents the logic of a control module of some program or other procedure named PROCESS_A_TRANS, which invokes lower-level modules such as GET_A_TRANS, passing parameters to them where appropriate (implied by SENDING), and receiving the parameters which they return (implied by RETURNING). The logic includes a loop and a branching decision.

A structure chart shows a picture of the hierarchy of modules which are invoked in a program or other piece of software.   The Yourdon/Constantine notation shown on the next page (Ref 6-3) is the most widely used.

6.4.1 Yourdon/Constantine

The invocation structure implied by the pseudo-code above would be shown like this:

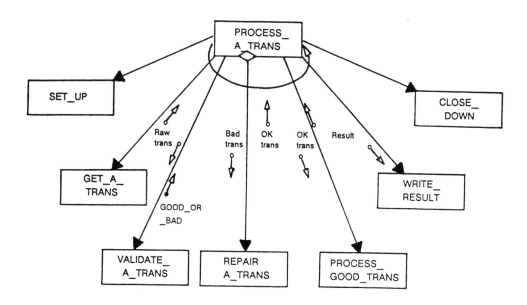

The sequence of placement of modules across the page has no necessary relationship to the sequence in which they will be invoked, though it makes the structure chart more meaningful if it can be read from left to right.

Parameters which are data elements or structures (e.g. RAW_TRANS) are shown with open circles on their tails, thus:

Parameters which are control flags (e.g. GOOD_OR_BAD) are shown with filled-in circles on their tails:

The presence of a loop is shown by putting the loop symbol round the invocation arrows involved.

Conditional invocation (e.g. in the case of REPAIR_A_TRANS) is shown by the small diamond.

6.4.2 Jackson

Michael Jackson (Ref 6-4) uses a technique that shows repetition and optionality, but does not show the parameters passed between modules:

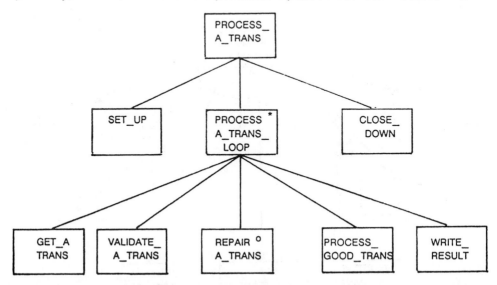

Modules which are iterated are marked with "*," while modules which are optionally invoked as part of a selection are marked with "o."

Both the Yourdon/Constantine technique and the Jackson technique are used to get a clean modular design before programming. The Yourdon/Constantine method of structured design starts from a detailed data flow diagram and shows how to derive a structure chart from it in such a way as to have a highly changeable modular design. This is important when the system is going to be implemented in a procedural language, such as COBOL or C, where the programmer can control the invocation structure for well or ill. It is less applicable when a 4GL or application generator is to be used.

References

Ref 6-1 Gane, C., and Sarson, T. *Structured Systems Analysis: Tools and Techniques.* Englewood Cliffs, NJ: Prentice-Hall, 1979

Ref 6-2 Martin, J., and McClure, C. *Action Diagrams: Clearly Structured Program Design.* Englewood Cliffs, NJ: Prentice-Hall, 1985

Ref 6-3 Yourdon, E., and Constantine, L. *Structured Design.* Englewood Cliffs, NJ: Prentice-Hall, 1979

Ref 6-4 Jackson, M. A. *Principles of Program Design.* London: Academic Press, 1975

Chapter 7

Code generation

Given a repository of data structures and elements, with definitions of physical files/databases, and a set of action diagrams that precisely describe the logic to be implemented in a program, it is a computable task to generate correct code in any chosen language.

To take a very simple example, given this action diagram:

```
|--Compute hypotenuse of right triangle--
|
|   Compute square of length of Side 1
|   Compute square of length of Side 2
|   Compute sum of squares
|   Compute square root of sum
|                giving length of hypotenuse
|--
```

and these repository entries:

	Physical name
length of side 1	ADJACENT
length of side 2	OPPOSITE
length of hypotenuse	HYPOTENUSE

the reader might like to consider the steps involved in converting it to the BASIC statements:

```
1000 REM   |--COMPUTE HYPOTENUSE OF RIGHT TRIANGLE--
1010 REM   |
1020 REM   |   COMPUTE SQUARE OF LENGTH OF SIDE 1
1030 REM   |   COMPUTE SQUARE OF LENGTH OF SIDE 2
1040 REM   |   COMPUTE SUM OF SQUARES
1050 REM   |   COMPUTE SQUARE ROOT OF SUM
1060 REM   |                GIVING LENGTH OF HYPOTENUSE
1070 REM   |--
1100   TEMP1 = ADJACENT * ADJACENT
1110   TEMP2 = OPPOSITE * OPPOSITE
1120   TEMP3 = TEMP1 + TEMP2
1130   HYPOTENUSE = SQR(TEMP3)
```

or converting it into any other language, such as C or COBOL.

More interestingly, it is clear that once the layout of a screen has been established, with literals specified and the data areas tagged to data elements in a repository, much of the screen-handling logic can be generated automatically. Indeed, if the data areas can be tagged to columns in a relational database, an application generator can automatically write software to insert, update, and delete values in the database, and can create a generalized query routine.

As an example of the type of facility available, we shall review the ORACLE Corporation's product, SQL*FORMS, which is a powerful generator, though not treated as a CASE product in this report.

7.1   A default application generator

Suppose you have created, in a database managed by the ORACLE relational database manager, a table called, say, PRODUCTS. Suppose this table contains four columns: one for a code which identifies each product, one for the name of each item, one for its description, and one for the product's price. You have done this by issuing the CREATE TABLE statement:

```
CREATE TABLE PRODUCTS        ...   The name you are giving the table is "PRODUCTS."
   ( CODE CHAR(4) NOT NULL,  ...   Since CODE is the key identifier, you don't want it
                                   ever to be missing; defining it as NOT NULL
                                   means that a value must be provided for every row.
   ITEM CHAR(12),            ...   Note each column and data-type is separated by a comma.
   DESCRIPTION CHAR(15),
   PRICE NUMBER(5,2) );      ...   This means five positions in all, with two decimal places.
```

The table exists, but it is empty; you have not inserted any data into it.

What you would like to do is to write a program that would allow you to insert product data through the screen, to change the PRODUCTS table, and to query the table without writing lengthy SELECT statements. How long would you expect it would take you to write such a program? With SQL*FORMS it can be done in about one minute.

Once a table like PRODUCTS has been created, you can load the SQL*FORMS software and say that you want to create a new application, which you will call, say, PRICING. You will then be shown a menu from which you can choose to create a custom screen or set up a default screen.

If you choose the default screen, you will be asked to supply the table name (PRODUCTS in this case), and asked to say how many rows you would like to see on the screen at any one time.

You can choose which columns from PRODUCTS you want to see displayed; if you take the default, they will all appear on the screen. You now return to the main menu and select the GENERATE option; SQL*FORMS goes to work and, using built-in rules, writes a program which will allow you to maintain and query the PRODUCTS table.

After a few seconds processing, SQL*FORMS responds:

```
Creation of application PRICING completed
```

and displays its main menu. To run PRICING, you select the "RUN" option and enter the name PRICING.

You will then be shown a screen that SQL*FORMS has generated using its built-in logic, like this:

```
                         ========  PRODUCTS  ========

    CODE      ITEM           DESCRIPTION      PRICE
```

You'll note that SQL*FORMS has used the table name as the header for the screen, and has used the column names that you gave in the CREATE TABLE statement as the column headings (which are stored in the data dictionary), allowing two spaces between each field. If the total of the column widths had been such that they would not all fit on one line, SQL*FORMS would have defaulted to displaying just one record on the screen, with two fields per line.

As well as doing this simple-minded screen layout for you (note that SQL*FORMS is not smart enough to space the four columns across the screen, but crams them to the left), it has generated (without your seeing it) all the logic needed to insert, change, and query data in the PRODUCTS table.

If you enter the details of several products on the screen (using function keys to go from column to column and from row to row) and then press the COMMIT key ("End" on a PC keyboard), this automatically generated code will create an INSERT statement for each row.

If you then press the Enter Query key (F1 on the PC; each terminal has a different set of function key assignments), tab across to the ITEM column and enter Pliers, you are setting up a query that is just the same as entering:

SELECT * FROM PRODUCTS WHERE ITEM = ' Pliers ' ;

When you press the Execute Query key (F2 on the PC), the application will retrieve and display the rows that meet the implied conditions you have set up, perhaps like this:

```
                              ========  PRODUCTS  ========

    CODE      ITEM          DESCRIPTION        PRICE

    T177      Pliers        Long nose          8.19
    T179      Pliers        Electrical         9.95
```

If you press Enter Query again, the data area will be blanked out, allowing a new query to be entered. You can enter combinations of conditions by, for example, entering Paintbrush under ITEM, and >3 under PRICE. This will produce a display of the paintbrushes selling for more than $3, the same as would have been produced by entering the query:

SELECT * FROM PRODUCTS WHERE ITEM = ' Paintbrush ' AND PRICE > 3

If you press Enter Query and then Execute Query without entering any conditions, you will get a listing of the whole table.

To update, for example, the price of a product, you first execute a query to get that product's row on the screen, then simply move the cursor to the entry, type in the new price, and then press the Commit key to commit the new value to the database.

So with a couple of dozen keystrokes, you have generated an application that carries out routine maintenance on the PRODUCTS table. The whole process takes a minute or two (once the table is created, which might take another minute). The logic of the default application which is created for you can be summed up in this action diagram:

```
Select RUN option from main menu

|--IF you want to INSERT data into the table
|     Press "Create New Record" key (See map for your keyboard)
|     Enter values for each column (Press "Next Field" key
|        to go from column to column)
|     (Press Down Arrow to enter a new record)
|     Press the "Commit" key to insert record(s) into database
|
|--ELSE  IF you want to QUERY the table
|     Press "Enter Query" key
|     Enter values (with or without comparison operators)
|        in each relevant column
|     Press the "Execute Query" key
|     IF query returns no records, press "Abort Query" key
|
|--ELSE  IF you want to UPDATE the table
|     Enter a query (as above) to display the records that
|        need to be updated
|     Use the "Next Field" key and Up/Down arrows to put the
|        cursor on each value to be changed
|     Type in the new value
|     Press the "Commit" key to change the record(s)
|        in the database
|
|--ELSE (you want to DELETE data from the table)
|     Enter a query (as above) to display the records that
|        need to be deleted
|     Use the Up/Down arrows to put the cursor on a row
|        to be deleted
|     Press the "Delete Record" key
|     Press the "Commit" key to actually delete the record(s)
|        from the database
|
|--END CASE
```

Of course, this application is quite crude: you may not like the default screen layout, or the screen heading, or the column headings. If you want to change them, this can be done quickly with the screen-painter facility.

7.2   A screen-painter

To use the screen-painter, you choose MODIFY from the main menu, and name the "form" you want to work on, in this case PRICING. The screen is displayed; you can change any of the headings by moving the cursor to the one you want to change, and typing in the new heading.

To move a field (perhaps you want to center the four fields on the screen), you place the cursor on the field, press the Select key, move the cursor to the new position, and press the Move key.

To add a new field (maybe Quantity in Stock), you move the cursor to the place where the field is to start, press Select, then move to the place where the field is to end, and press Select again. Then you press the Create Field key. SQL*FORMS will then display a "pop-up" area on the screen like this:

```
 _____
|                                                |
|        DEFINE FIELD            Seq # ___        |
| Name _____|
| Data type:                                     |
|    CHAR      NUMBER      RNUMBER      DATE       |
|    ALPHA     INT         RINT        JDATE       |
|              MONEY       RMONEY       EDATE      |
| Actions:                                        |
|    SQL       ATTRIBUTES         VALIDATION       |
|_____|
```

You enter the sequence # for the new field (5 in this case if it is to be to the right of the existing 4 fields), and enter its name. Then you select the data type from the options presented (several of which are specific to ORACLE). In this case you would select RINT to get a right-justified integer field.

If you now put the cursor on ATTRIBUTES, SQL*FORMS will display another pop-up like the one on the following page:

```
| SPECIFY ATTRIBUTES  |
|   Database Field    | - field on screen corresponds to a field in database
|   Primary Key       | - this field is (part of) the primary key of the table
|                     |
|   Displayed         | - the field will appear on the screen (fields can be defined but invisible)
|   Input allowed     | - you can enter data with this field
|   Update allowed    | - you can change data retrieved into this field by a query
|   Fixed length      | - the value you enter must be exactly as long as the field
|   Mandatory         | - the field cannot be left blank
|   Uppercase         | - lowercase letters will be converted on entry
|   Autoskip          | - when a fixed length field is full,
|                     |     the cursor will jump to the next field
```

You select the options that apply to the Quantity In Stock field.   In this case it will be a field in the database (you should alter the table to add an IN_STOCK_QTY column), but will not be the primary key.   It will be displayed; you want to be able to enter values and to change values if they are not correct. It cannot be fixed length, and probably should be made mandatory (if you enter a new product, you should enter the quantity in stock, even if it's zero). "Uppercase" and "autoskip" are irrelevant for this field.

When you have selected the attributes that should apply, you press the Accept key to store your choices, and SQL*FORMS will display the DEFINE FIELD pop-up again.   From this, you should next select the VALIDATION action, which will show a pop-up like this:

```
|         SPECIFY VALIDATION           |
| Field Length 4_   Query Length ___   | - specify if different from the length selected
| KEY Block _____   |
| COPY Fld  _____   | - if the field value can be copied from elsewhere
| DEFAULT   _____   | - if you want a standard (changeable)
| RANGE Low _____   |                    default value to be displayed
|      High _____   | - for editing
| LIST  Tab _____   |  -}
|    Column _____   |    } if a list of values can be found in some table
| HELP:                                |  }
| Enter value for: QTY_IN_STOCK        | - the message the operator will see if
```
- the message the operator will see if
  he presses the Help key.
  This is the default message, but you
  can supply any 80-character message you
  want, and optionally have it automatically
  displayed at the bottom of the screen
  whenever the cursor enters the field, thus
  giving the operator quite detailed prompts.

This pop-up enables you to specify how the field should be edited, plus some other characteristics. In this case, there is no relevant DEFAULT that should be placed in the field every time the screen is displayed; DEFAULT is useful when, for example, 98% of all transactions are for cash, so that a default value of "Cash" in the HOW_PAID field would need to be overridden only 2% of the time.

If you specify a RANGE, then values outside that range will be rejected.

Once the VALIDATION options have been selected, you press the Accept key to return to the DEFINE FIELD pop-up. Lastly, you could select the SQL action to enter a SQL statement that would be executed when this field was changed.

For example, if you wanted to have the ITEM, DESCRIPTION, and PRICE displayed whenever you entered a product code (without pressing any query keys), you would attach to the CODE field the statement:

SELECT ITEM, DESCRIPTION, PRICE
   INTO ITEM, DESCRIPTION, PRICE   (field names in an INTO clause refer to screen fields)
     FROM PRODUCTS
       WHERE CODE = &CODE   (&CODE means "the value of the CODE field
                                  entered on the screen")

In the case of IN_STOCK_QTY, no SQL statement is relevant, so you press Accept again, and are returned to the screen-painter with all your choices for the new field stored in the database, along with the modified screen definition.

(For more details of the field definition options, see Ref 7-1.)

If you wanted to create a completely custom screen from scratch, of course, you would follow a similar procedure for all the fields on the screen. The screen-painter also enables you to draw boxes and lines, so that you can improve the clarity of the display.

7.3 Where's the source code?

SQL*FORMS has many more facilities than have been mentioned in this brief review. As well as attaching SQL statements to fields, as we just discussed, fields can be grouped into blocks (areas of the screen each accessing a different table), and SQL statements can be triggered when a block is used for a query, insert, update, or delete. IF statements can be attached to fields or blocks to allow branching logic (with its attendant debugging problems!).

SQL*FORMS is not the only such rapid application generation facility. Relational Technology Inc. markets a very comparable product, Applications-By-Forms (ABF) for use with their INGRES relational DBMS.

At the time of writing, there seems to be no language of comparable power available for users of DB2.

Both SQL*FORMS and ABF can be described as "visual programming" tools. The specification of screen display and processing is done while looking at the resultant screen itself, not by the conventional process of changing source code, compiling, running, and only then seeing the consequences of the source code changes. Visual programming is a powerful aid to rapid development.

Both SQL*FORMS and ABF store the "source code" (the field locations, options, and SQL statements) in tables in the relational databases (ORACLE and INGRES, respectively). These tables can be listed out if required, but source code is less important with a visual programming tool than with a conventional language. If you want to change a screen layout, don't go to the source code; instead, bring up the screen in question, and use the screen-painter. If you want to change a SQL statement, go to the field in question, invoke the SQL action in the DEFINE FIELD pop-up, and change the SQL statement displayed. You need to see a listing only if there is a series of SQL statements associated with a field or a block and you want to think through what will happen as each is executed.

It's noteworthy, also, that these visual programming tools generate machine language (on whatever hardware they run on) rather than COBOL or any other third-generation language. Consequently, there is no need to maintain the procedural logic; it is all attached to the screens of the system.

At least for broad classes of on-line business systems, it may be that the death of COBOL, news of which has so frequently been exaggerated, is finally at hand.

Information about SQL*FORMS is available from:

ORACLE Corporation
20 Davis Drive
Belmont, CA 94002
800/345-DBMS

Information about APPLICATIONS-BY-FORMS is available from:

Relational Technology Inc.
1080 Marina Village Parkway
Alameda, CA 94501
415/769-1400

Reference

7-1   Gane, C.   *Developing Business Systems in SQL using ORACLE on the IBM PC.*   New York: Rapid System Development Inc., 1986

Chapter 8

Project Management
Support - IPSE

Up until now in Part I, we have considered primarily technical aspects of system development. Besides this, there are many areas of project planning and control where automated help can be of value. These areas include:

- Project planning and estimating

- On-line access to system development methodology and standards

- Project document control and version control

- Time accounting, event recording, and status reporting

- Problem recording and tracking

Each of these areas is discussed in detail in this chapter.

Many CASE products do not provide significant help in these areas. Products that concentrate on such project management support (with or without supporting analysis/design) have become known as IPSE (Integrated Project Support Environment) products; the best known IPSE product is possibly Softlab's MAESTRO.

8.1   Project planning and estimating

At the start of a project, one of the project manager's jobs is to list the tasks to be completed in the project, specify the deliverables to be produced, establish how many people are going to work on the project and when, decide what other resources will be needed, and combine all this into estimates of cost and calendar time.

To do this, the project manager needs:

1.   a task list. A standard task list can be provided for the project manager to customize, or the project manager can insert his or her own tasks into e.g. a spreadsheet.

2.   information on task interdependencies, for example, that the database cannot be loaded before it has been created.

3.   hourly or daily charging rates for the people involved, and for other resources.

4.   a calendar showing vacations, commitments of people to other activities, space availability, committed delivery dates, and so on.

Estimates can be arrived at in two ways: by rolling up detail and by global comparison.

To roll up detail, the project manager needs to be able to combine many statements like "Program 346 will take Joe 50 hours at $38 per hour, and he can't start until July 1 and July 4 is a vacation, so I estimate he'll finish on ..."

To make global comparisons, the project manager needs a database of many past projects with data about their cost and the time they took, correlated with such factors as the number of user departments to be served by the system, the experience of the people available, how long the software to be used has been on the market, and so on.

8.2   On-line access to a system development methodology and standards

The simplest kind of methodology is a list of tasks to be performed,   for example:

Task 1:   Define the users to be served by the system.
Task 2:   Define the scope of the system required, etc.

A system development methodology (SDM) contains not only a task list but also for each task a detailed description of:

- when it should be done
- what techniques should be used
- what should be produced by the task
- who should perform the task
- sub-tasks within the task

Together with the task dependencies, this forms a task model, which can be either documented in a reference manual or made available at a workstation. Thus an analyst, perhaps, might query the task model to see what needs to be done next on the project, and might be told by the system "Task 76: normalize the data structures." The available options might be to list the data structures already defined, use the normalization dialog (see Chapter 5), see a detailed description of Task 76, or engage in an on-line tutorial on normalization.

As well as the task model, an SDM should define deliverables. Thus every Requirements Statement produced in an organization should follow a common table of contents (sensibly customized). It is convenient to have such a model for each deliverable available at the workstation, with help available on what is required under each heading.

8.3   Project document control and version control

In the course of a project, many documents are evolved and go through multiple versions. Some of the documents are pure text (such as a Feasibility Study), some combine text and graphics (such as a Requirements Statement using DFDs and ERDs), while some contain just source code. Several facilities are useful.

Controlled access

It can be very valuable to have all documents on-line to a number of workstations, perhaps at different locations. Analysts in Tokyo, New York, and London can all see the latest version of a document produced by any one of them. But shared access needs to be controlled, both for reading and for changing.

In many environments, anyone authorized to use a workstation can read any project document. However, some parts of some documents may be sensitive, such as individual hourly cost rates or product profitability. Consequently, it may be desirable either to have different classes of readers, or to establish a distribution list for each document, with the document creator specifying explicitly who is to be allowed to read it, and who should get a copy for review.

Control of updating needs to be maintained, so that someone trying to change a document sees the very latest version, and does not change something that another worker is also in the process of changing. Consequently, there needs to be a locking mechanism, such that if an authorized person starts to change, for example, a DFD, then that DFD is locked for update until the person has finished making the change. While it is locked, any authorized person can look at it, but anyone trying to make a change will be told that it is locked, when it was locked, and who locked it.

Comment markup

Often, a draft of a document is produced for review by several different people, perhaps at different locations.   Rather than have them write their comments, each on a copy, and return all those copies to the originator, it is convenient for them to be able to enter their comments at a workstation, and for the originator to then be able to call up (or print out) the document with all the various comments (with initials and a date-time stamp automatically added), tagged to the relevant section.

Version control

A document may go through many versions during the life of the system. Normally, as changes are made, the previous version is overwritten, so only the latest version exists in machine-readable form (though various earlier hard-copy versions, often undated, may be spread around the organization).   This poses a problem if, for any reason, it is necessary to back-off to a previous version, or if it is desirable to trace the sequence of events which led to the current version.

Version control may be achieved either by storing every version of every document (which makes heavy demands on storage), or by storing the latest version plus all the changes that have led to it.   To take a trivial example:

Version 1:		The quick brown fox jumped over the lazy dog.
	Change 1:	*(April 1)* Substitute "fox" for "quick brown fox"
Version 2:		The fox jumped over the lazy dog.
	Change 2:	*(April 3)* Substitute "moon" for "lazy dog"
Version 3:		The fox jumped over the moon.
	Change 3:	*(April 5)* Substitute "cow" for "fox"
Current version:		The cow jumped over the moon.

If we now delete all previous versions:

Change 1:   *(April 1)*   Substitute "fox" for "quick brown fox"
Change 2:   *(April 3)*   Substitute "moon" for "lazy dog"
Change 3:   *(April 5)*   Substitute "cow" for "fox"

Current version: The cow jumped over the moon.

By working back through the changes, it is still possible to tell what the version was on April 2. A version control facility automates this process, and also keeps track of who made each change, perhaps with that person's comment as to why it was made.

Reusable code library

Where reusable modules, or screen templates, or model reports have been identified, they can be placed in the document library for access by authorized users.

8.4   Time accounting, event recording, and status reporting

As people work on tasks within a project, the hours they expend can be charged to the appropriate task. Whether the task structure is coarse (e.g., "Analysis," "Design,") or fine (e.g., "Task 76: normalize data structures"), it is useful for the project manager to get reports comparing estimated time with actual time expended. Perhaps even more valuable is a report of "current estimated time to complete." (One school of project management holds that the original estimate, and the actual to-date, are already ancient history; what actually matters for project control is each person's honest estimate of how long they're truly going to take from now to complete what they're working on.)

As well as estimated and actual times, the project manager needs to be able to capture and display the occurrence of events. Good project management breaks a complex project down into as many mini-milestones as feasible. For example, if a user signs off on the prototype of a data entry dialog, that may be the end-point of a task, and thus a recordable event. Knowing whether or not definable events have occurred is often more important than having estimates of percentage completion on tasks.

Once estimates and actual times, and estimated and actual event dates, have been captured in the system, a large variety of meaningful status reports can be generated, in both narrative and graphic form.

8.5   Problem recording and tracking

One facility that applies not only to development but also to maintenance and operations is that of centralized problem tracking. Whenever anyone working on the project becomes aware of a problem, such as an incomplete definition, or an inconsistency, or user feedback that a requirement is not being met, it should be entered into the central problem database, with a date-time stamp and the recorder's ID. Ideally, the existing problems in the database should be scanned to see whether this is a known problem or whether it is similar to a known problem (and if so, whether there is a known solution).

Problems can then be grouped and routed to the best person for their resolution, who records the action taken and whether the problem is resolved or is still outstanding. Problems can also be graded (e.g. as critical, important, nice-to-fix, and so on). This enables the project manager to query the database to see, for example, how many critical problems still remain to be resolved by the users, in order of the time elapsed since they were logged.

Chapter 9

Step-by-step approaches to system development/maintenance

In Section 8.2, we described a system development methodology (SDM) as consisting of at least a step-by-step description of the tasks required to plan, specify, design, and implement a system. An SDM should also include a detailed definition of the deliverables to be produced, and guidance as to which member(s) of the project should be involved in each task.

Many SDMs have been developed, some for internal use in organizations, some available for license supported by consulting firms. Most of those which are relevant to the use of CASE products fall into two broad classes, Information Engineering or Structured Systems Engineering.

9.1   Information Engineering (IE)

IE is a planning and development methodology associated with James Martin (Ref 9-1) and the firm of Arthur Young (Ref 9-2).

Several variants have been described; the version of IE used by Arthur Young specifies four main phases:

Information Systems Planning (ISP).   During ISP, the team examines the business plans of the organization, and analyzes senior management's view of goals and Critical Success Factors (CSFs). An Enterprise Information Model is produced, and the enterprise is divided into Business Areas. A 3-5 year Information Systems Plan is developed.

Business Area Analysis (BAA).   For each Business Area defined in ISP, a logical model is developed describing data flow, data content, and business policy. Various design alternatives are examined, and an implementation approach is chosen.

System Design.   The requirements established in BAA are used to produce detailed system specifications; interactive dialogs may be prototyped.

Construction.   Code is generated (or written) and tested, users are trained in operation, and the system is implemented.

Each of these phases consists of defined activities, using various techniques to produce defined deliverables.

The description of Information Engineering given in the next few pages is adapted from Ref. 9-2, with acknowledgments to Arthur Young & Company.

Information Systems Planning

<u>Activities:</u>	Techniques used (other than text):
▪ Organize and control Information Systems Planning Project	*Project planning*
▪ Define Enterprise Business Strategy	*Decomposition diag.* *(organization chart)*
▪ Develop Initial Enterprise Information Model	*Decomposition diag., ERD, Matrices* *e.g. Business Functions vs. Critical* *Success Factors*
▪ Develop Detailed Enterprise Information Model	*Decomposition diag., ERD,* *Matrices*
▪ Profile Existing Information Systems	*Matrices e.g. systems* *vs. processes*
▪ Create Information Needs Report	
▪ Develop Information Systems Plan	
▪ Perform Project Approval and Assessment Tasks	

<u>ISP Deliverables:</u>

▪ Information Needs Report (A consolidated statement of the information needs of executive management, line management, and the MIS organization)	
▪ Enterprise Information Model	*ERD, Decomposition diag.,* *matrices*
▪ Information Systems Profile Report (An inventory of existing systems, data, and other resources.)	
▪ Information Systems Plan (A prioritized set of project definitions, with development schedule)	

Business Area Analysis

Activities:

Techniques used
(other than text):

- Organize and control Business
  Area Analysis Project

Project planning

- Define Business Area and Business
  Area Partitions

*Clustering of CSFs,
Business functions, etc.*

- Model Existing Business Area Partition

- Model Future Business Area Partition

*ERD, DFD, Matrices,
Decomposition diag. (for
processes), Prototyping,
Action diag., normalization*

- Document Technical Requirements

- Determine Business Area Implementation
  Approach

- Perform Project Approval and
  Assessment Tasks

BAA Deliverables:

- Business Area Information Model

ERD, Normalization, Action diag.

- Business Area Requirements

- Business Area Technical Requirements
  Report

- Enterprise Benefits Analysis

- Business Area Implementation Approach
  (Initial high-level system design)

System Design

Activities:	Techniques used (other than text):
■ Organize and control System Design Project	
■ Determine Technology Support	
■ Design Cultural Changes	
■ Design Externals	*Prototyping, action diag.*
■ Design Database	*ERD, normalization, data navigation diag.*
■ Design Internals	*DFD, structure chart, action diag.*
■ Design Conversion System	
■ Design System Tests	
■ Design Training Program	
■ Perform Project Approval and Assessment Tasks	

System Design Deliverables:

■ Detail System Design

■ User Reference
(Interface prototypes, manual
procedures, organizational changes, etc.)

■ Conversion System Design

■ System Test Design

■ Training Program Design

Construction

Activities:	Techniques used (other than text):

Activities:

Techniques used (other than text):

- Organize and control Construction Project

  Project planning

- Prepare Construction and Test Environment

- Implement Design Specifications

  Action diag., code generation

- Implement Development Product

- Implement Application Package

- Compile Documentation

  Design database/Repository

- Develop and Conduct Training Program

- Test System

- Install System and Turn Over to Users

- Perform Project Approval and Assessment Tasks

Construction Deliverables:

- System Documentation Package

- Operational Database

- Installed Operational System

- System Operating Procedures

- Training Program

9.2 Structured Systems Engineering (SSE)

SSE is a generic term covering several SDMs based around the use of structured analysis and design techniques. The proprietary SDMs STRADIS (STRuctured Analysis Design and Implementation of Information Systems), marketed by McDonnell Douglas, and LSDM (LBMS Structured Development Methodology), marketed by Learmonth and Burchett Management Systems, are well-known examples of this approach.

SSE recommends the development and maintenance of a Strategic Information Systems plan, but does not depend on its existence, recognizing that many organizations do not have a management culture that will support strategic planning. SSE distinguishes 6 phases:

Strategic Information Systems Planning (SISP). Where top management support can be gained, each Strategic Business Unit is studied to see how information technology can be used to gain a strategic advantage, and to decide which systems should be built over the planning period, in what sequence. Systems are identified by studying a DFD that covers the entire Strategic Business Unit, and partitioning the DFD into systems which, other things being equal, have the simplest interfaces between them.

Requirements Analysis. For each system defined in SISP, or for each new development request that meets the criteria for a profitable project, a logical model is developed, consisting of a system-wide DFD and ERD, a data definition repository, and action diagrams for each process. Various outline physical designs are considered (with some prototyping if appropriate), and a chosen design is identified.

System Design. The database, software units, and manual procedures are specified in the detail appropriate to the target implementation environment. (If the action diagrams from requirements analysis are to be converted directly to code, no process design may be needed.) While design is proceeding, test data and predicted outputs are developed.

Implementation. Top-down implementation is used, starting with the development of a skeleton version, which does the minimum necessary to exercise interfaces, and adding data and function to the skeleton through a series of versions, until the full system is in place. The necessary code is generated or written, dialogs are exercised with representative users and then revised, databases are created and loaded, conversion bridges are written, and each version is tested until a fully working tuned system is ready to be installed.

Installation. User training is completed, the working system is installed on the hardware, databases are converted for live running, and the users accept the system.

Maintenance. SSE prescribes an organized approach to maintenance, in which urgent problems are fixed, and non-urgent ones are grouped into regular releases of tested versions of the system.

Strategic Information Systems Planning (SISP)

Activities:	Techniques used (other than text):
▪ Review business strategy; identify business units for which an SISP is to be developed, and form team for each unit	*Decomposition diag.*
▪ Survey user problems, requirements and ideas for use of IS	
▪ Develop DFD for each strategic planning unit	*DFD*
▪ Develop ERD for each strategic planning unit	*ERD*
▪ Survey competitive environment	
▪ Assess technology future for business and IS	
▪ Develop ideal system architecture (databases, systems, network)	
▪ Assess nature and quality of existing and "committed-to-build" systems	
▪ Determine sequence of system development and plan to "get there from here"	

SISP deliverables

▪ Logical model of strategic business unit	*DFD, ERD*
▪ Strategic Information Systems Plan (Prioritized projects, related to logical model)	

Requirements Analysis

If no SISP exists, review each request for new system development, to establish likely benefits and ROI.

Where system is to be built as part of SISP, or where system receives funding from appropriate management group:

Activities:	Techniques used (other than text):
■ Develop DFD for system area	*DFD*
■ Develop ERD for system area	*ERD*
■ Establish problems with current situation, objectives for new system, constraints on the project	
■ Develop alternative outline designs - choose best	
■ Refine DFD, ERD; produce normalized data structures; document repository for chosen alternative	*DFD, ERD, Normalization, Design database/repository*
■ Exercise prototypes of selected dialogs	*Prototyping*
■ Produce Requirements Statement, and document Outline Physical Design	

RA deliverables

■ Requirements Statement
(Logical model of system, plus objectives and constraints)

■ Outline Physical Design
(related to logical model)

System Design

<u>Activities:</u>

Techniques used
(other than text):

- Partition system DFD into software
procedure units

  DFD

- Design physical database

- Decide which procedures are to be
developed by prototyping

- Produce logic specifications for programs
where required

  *Action diags.,
  Structure chart*

- Draft user procedures

- Develop test case specifications

- Develop top-down implementation plan

- Produce Design Statement

<u>SD deliverables</u>

- Partitioned DFD

  DFD

- Physical database design and DDL

- Structure charts for those programs to be
implemented in a procedural language

  Structure chart

- Implementation plan with test plan for
each version

Implementation

Activities:

Techniques used (other than text):

- Generate/write code for each procedure

Code generation

- Exercise dialogs with representative users and revise

Prototyping

- Produce user manuals and training

- Test each version

- Load database and tune for performance

Implementation deliverables

- Requirements Statement and Design Statement (as revised)

- Production library and program documentation

- Database definition statements

- Test data and test outputs

- User manuals

- User training documentation

- Operator manuals

Installation

Activities:

Techniques used
(other than text):

- Install any hardware required

- Train users

- Convert database for live running

- Carry out parallel testing if planned

- Hand over system to operations and
  maintenance teams

Installation deliverables:

Accepted, documented system

Maintenance

Techniques used
(other than text):

Activities:

- Determine cause of reported problem
  (e.g. misuse of system, DBMS error)

- Determine urgency

- Fix urgent problems

- Incorporate patches and non-urgent changes
  into next release

- Code and test new release of system

Maintenance deliverables:

Urgent fix: Patched system, plus specification of
upgrade for next release

New release of accepted, documented system

9.3 The convergence of IE and SSE

From the previous two sections, we can see that the similarities between IE and SSE are greater than their differences. The principal difference is that IE centers around an entity-relationship model as the key tool, whereas SSE centers around a data flow model. Indeed, early versions of IE (such as that implemented in TI's IEF) made no use of DFDs, and some early versions of SSE made no use of ERDs.

Interestingly enough, though, as practitioners of both approaches have gained experience, they have come to realize that both DFDs and ERDs are necessary for a full understanding of the system. A DFD is necessary to show how the processes and the data in the system fit together, and how the whole area can best be partitioned into systems or programs with the fewest data flows crossing their boundaries. An ERD is necessary to show how the data entities of the area fit together, and to provide a baseline for database design.

IE builds an ERD first and then creates a DFD based on that understanding of the data. SSE builds a DFD first and then builds an ERD from the data stores. While advocates of each position feel very strongly about the matter, there are advantages and disadvantages to each side. Possibly some situations lend themselves more naturally to starting with an ERD (for example, where a lot is known about the data to be stored, but little is known about inputs, outputs, and processes). Others may lend themselves better to starting with a DFD (for example, where the scope of the system needs to be strictly defined, and a lot is known about inputs and outputs).

So it seems likely that CASE tools in the future will support both methodologies, and that we shall see a convergence to a *de facto* industry standard, on which almost all practitioners agree.

References

Ref 9-1 Martin, J., and Hershey E. *Information Engineering, a Management White Paper,* published by Knowledgeware Inc., 1986.

Ref 9-2 Arthur Young's *Practical Guide to Information Engineering,* New York: John Wiley, 1987.

Chapter 10

Market analysis

To give some feel for the size and structure of the CASE marketplace, we give here a survey of 1987/1988 revenues and unit sales for the products covered in Part III, with 1989 projections at the time of writing.

The first thing that strikes one about the CASE marketplace is its degree of fragmentation. Though EXCELERATOR remains the leading front-end modelling product, doubling its 1987 revenue of some $20 million to a projected $40 million in 1989, at the end of which it will likely have sold some 25,000 copies, its share of the total market was less than 20% in 1987 and will likely fall to perhaps 10% in 1989 (Table 1).

Indeed, if the projections used here turn out to be anywhere near accurate, only EXCELERATOR, TEAMWORK, and IEW will get more than 10% of the front-end sub-market in 1989. Apart from MAESTRO, whose growth is most remarkable, the 18 other vendors listed will achieve market shares in the single digits, though showing quite remarkable growth in many cases.

The overall growth of this segment of the software market is striking. The gross total revenue figures show a doubling from 1987 to 1988, and a further 50% increase in 1989 over 1988. If we consider just the front-end modelling group alone (i.e. omitting APS, CorVision, MAESTRO, TELON, and TRANSFORM), the growth figures are 76% and 73% respectively, with a total of nearly 100,000 copies of front-end products projected to be installed by the end of 1989.

How long can this rate of growth go on? We know that no tree grows to the sky, so it is prudent to consider if and when the profession will be saturated. After all, even if we consider a declining rate of growth such as this:

Year	% growth in revenue over previous year	Front-end revenues ($million)
1988	75%	$135m
1989	70%	$230m
1990	65%	$380m
1991	60%	$610m
1992	55%	$945m
1993	50%	$1,420m

it still suggests that the front-end CASE market will be larger than the DBMS market by the early 1990s.

Basis for revenue figures

Most vendors have been kind enough to supply figures for the number of units sold in 1987 and 1988, the total number of units or installations at the end of 1988, and their projected unit sales for 1989. Some vendors have been very open and helpful in translating those unit sales into approximate revenue dollars. Where it has not been possible for a vendor to release dollar figures, an estimate has been generated based on unit sales, on the first copy price of the product(s), and on industry practice in providing volume discounts. While, obviously, the relative number of single copy sales, multi-copy sales, site licenses, and other high-volume sales varies from vendor to vendor, typical experience seems to be that the average revenue per unit is about 50% of the first copy price. In other cases, an estimate of revenue based on industry sources has been given.

Where the phrase "Approx..." has been used in discussing the market share of each product, the estimate is probably in error by no more than $+/-$ 25%. Thus a figure of "Approx. $10 million" may actually be anywhere between $7.5 million and $12.5 million.
Where the phrase "In the $n million range" is used, the estimate may be in error by $+/-$ 50% or more. Thus a figure "in the $10 million range" may actually be anywhere between $5 million and $15 million.

For purposes of the comparative tables on the next few pages, all figures have been treated as being equally reliable, and where a range of estimates has been given in the product description, the mid-point of that range has been used to provide a single figure (admittedly an artificial one). Consequently, **no reliance should be placed on the figures in Tables 1 and 2 for any purpose, other than a purely indicative one.**

Table 1: 1987-89 CASE total market estimates by product line

Product	Vendor	Units shipped 1987	Revenue ($mil) 1987	% total market 1987	Units shipped 1988	Revenue ($mil) 1988	% total market 1988	Units installed end-1988	Projected Units Shipped 1989	Projected revenue ($mil) 1989	% total Projected market 1989
AD/T	Yourdon	1000	2	1.7	2000	4	1.6	3000	2000	4	1.0
ANATOOL	Advanced Logic	300	0.25	0.2	600	0.6	0.2	1000	1500	1.5	0.4
APS	Sage	53	10	8.3	75	15	6.1	200	90	17	4.4
BACHMAN	Bachman	0	0	0	100	2.5	1.0	100	300	10	2.6
CorVision	Cortex	70	7	5.8	120	12	4.9	1000	150	15	3.9
Deft	DEFT	50	0.5	0.4	125	1.3	0.5	425	250	2.5	0.7
DEVELOPER	Asyst	200	1	0.8	700	3.5	1.4	1000	1500	8	2.1
ERD	Chen	300	0.5	0.4	300	0.5	0.2	600	600	1	0.3
EXCELERATOR	Index Tech.	6500	22.9	19.0	8500	30	12.2	14000	11000	40	10.4
IEF	Texas Insts.	70	5*	4.2	50*	17.5	7.1	120	50	20*	5.2
IEW	Knowledgeware	3700	15*	12.5	4000	20*	8.1	10000	7000	40*	10.4
MAESTRO	Softlab	50	8	6.7	170	60	24.4	450	200	80	20.9
Meta Tools	Meta Systems	100	3	2.5	200	5	2.0	500	150	5	1.3
MULTI/CAM	AGS	480	1.75	1.5	300	2.1	0.9	650	400	3.5	0.9
ProKitWB	McDonnell Doug.	400	2.5	2.1	1000	6	2.4	1400	1500	8	2.1
SW/Picts	IDE	300	2	1.7	700	6	2.4	1200	1250	15	3.9
SYS ENGR	LBMS	1750	4*	3.3	2000	5*	2.0	4000	4000	10*	2.6
TEAMWORK	Cadre	1000	10*	8.3	2000	20*	8.1	4000	4000	40*	10.4
TELON	Pansophic	71	13	10.8	90	17.5	7.1	370	110	20	5.2
TRANSFORM	TRANSFORM	10	5	4.2	12	5	2.0	52	20	15	3.9
VAW	Visible Syst.	2300	4.1	3.4	4000	7	2.9	6300	8000	15	3.9
vsDesigner	Visual SW	550	2.75	2.3	1000	5	2.0	1500	2000	13	3.4
		19254	120.25	100	28042	245.5	100	51867	46070	383.5	100

Figures marked * are estimates of varying degrees of reliability.

Table 2: 1987-89 CASE market estimates: "Front-end" modelling products only.

Product	Vendor	Units shipped 1987	Revenue ($mil) 1987	% total market 1987	Units shipped 1988	Revenue ($mil) 1988	% total market 1988	Units installed end-1988	Projected Units Shipped 1989	Projected revenue ($mil) 1989	% total Projected market 1989
AD/T	Yourdon	1000	2	2.6	2000	4	2.9	3000	2000	4	1.7
ANATOOL	Advanced Logic	300	0.25	0.3	600	0.6	0.4	1000	1500	1.5	0.6
BACHMAN	Bachman	0	0	0	100	2.5	1.8	100	300	10	4.2
Deft	DEFT	50	0.5	0.6	125	1.3	1.0	425	250	2.5	1.1
DEVELOPER	Asyst	200	1	1.3	700	3.5	2.6	1000	1500	8	3.4
ERD	Chen	300	0.5	0.6	300	0.5	0.4	600	600	1	0.4
EXCELERATOR	Index Tech.	6500	22.9	29.6	8500	30	22.1	14000	11000	40	16.9
IEF	Texas Insts.	70	5	6.5	50	17.5	12.9	120	50	20	8.5
IEW	Knowledgeware	3700	15	19.4	4000	20	14.7	10000	7000	40	16.9
Meta Tools	Meta Systems	100	3	3.9	200	5	3.7	500	150	5	2.1
MULTI/CAM	AGS	480	1.75	2.3	300	2.1	1.5	650	400	3.5	1.5
ProKitWB	McDonnell Doug.	400	2.5	3.2	1000	6	4.4	1400	1500	8	3.4
SW/Picts	IDE	300	2	2.6	700	6	4.4	1200	1250	15	6.3
SYS ENGR	LBMS	1750	4	5.2	2000	5	3.7	4000	4000	10	4.2
TEAMWORK	Cadre	1000	10	12.9	2000	20	14.7	4000	4000	40	16.9
VAW	Visible Syst.	2300	4.1	5.3	4000	7	5.1	6300	8000	15	6.3
vsDesigner	Visual SW	550	2.75	3.6	1000	5	3.7	1500	2000	13	5.5
		19000	77.25	100	27575	136	100	49795	45500	236.5	100

Chapter 11
The future of CASE

11.1 What would be an ideal system development/maintenance environment?

In thinking about the future of CASE, it's useful to have an idea of where imaginable technical developments in cheap computer power and artificial intelligence techniques might take us.

We can look forward to each professional having a personal workstation with many MIPS and megabytes, and with a high-definition screen the size of a small drawing board, communicating with other workstations and mainframes over fiber-optic cables and the like, at much higher data-transfer rates than we are used to. We can expect expert systems that come close to the best human performance at tasks such as database design and performance optimization. We can look forward to natural-language parsers which can handle a wide vocabulary and range of syntactic structures, and which, when they don't understand us, will explain to us how to explain what we mean to them. Even if speaker-independent voice-recognition remains elusive, input will become easier for humans, through on-line typing-improvement games, self-correcting input analyzers (if I type "hte" before a noun, fix it, especially if it's a mistake I often make), and fluent pointing mechanisms (touch the screen with a magic pencil?)

Given such resources, we can expect to work with a system which is the same whether we are developing new software or maintaining existing software. (It has been said only half in jest that development is just a special case of maintenance!) This system development/maintenance environment (SDME) will:

- know all significant data elements/structures in all machine-readable files in the organization (possibly also those in use but not yet machine-readable). The SDME will know:

  - what each element/structure means and what depends on what
  - where the physical data is currently located
  - who's authorized to do what with any given piece of data

- know the function and text of all modules of code in any machine library anywhere in the organization, and have a catalog of those available from vendors.

- know me, what I'm authorized to do, and what my skills are (and are not!) so that it can tutor me where I'm weak and not bore me where I'm fluent.

- continuously optimize its own performance without human intervention except for policy (e.g. to what extent update-transaction response-time should be sacrificed to management ad hoc queries).   It would ask for more hardware when it needs it (e.g. "If you want me to keep up these response times with this rate of growth of transactions, then I'm going to need another 4 megabytes in three week's time...")

- have a natural-language requirements parser.

The natural-language requirements parser might enable someone in the role of analyst to build systems from scratch, or to build systems by modifying existing systems, or to maintain existing systems.   To take a possible dialog:

Analyst: *I want to extend the book sales system to handle seminar enrollments.*

SDME: *What's a seminar enrollment?*

Analyst: *A customer wants to attend a specific seminar for a specific fee.*

SDME: *By "customer" do you mean the same as a person who orders a book, as described in the existing table CUSTOMERS:*

                        .....
                        .....
                        .....

Analyst: *Yes, but a person who hasn't ordered a book can become a customer by enrolling in a seminar.*

SDME: *My thesaurus says that "seminar" has synonyms "course" and "workshop."   There are no data elements anywhere in the organization that describe any of these.   What data elements describe a specific seminar?*

Analyst: *(describes new data elements)*

SDME: *Based on what you've told me, I've generated a modified version of the book sales system.   Please exercise it and tell me if it is close to what you want, or whether we should design a new system from scratch.*

(Analyst exercises first-cut system with representative users.)

Analyst: *We need to see whether a customer previously bought the seminar text, because if so he gets a discount equal to the purchase price of the text.*

SDME: *Noted; from what you've told me I infer three normalized tables:*

SEMINARS	*PRESENTATIONS*	*ENROLLEES*
.....	.....	.....
.....	.....	.....
.....	.....	.....

Can you see any problem with these?

Analyst: *Looks good to me.*

SDME: *I'm sending a message to Datalord (the human database administrator) requesting permission to add these to the corporate database.*

(Phone rings)   *Jack Datalord here; if you identify a seminar presentation just by city and start date, will that always be unique?*

Analyst: *No, you've got a point.   (To SDME):   Add a 4-digit code to PRESENTATIONS as the unique identifier.*

SDME: *Then the PRESENTATIONS table will look like this:*

                    .....
                    .....
                    .....

I'm regenerating the application; do you want to see a data flow diagram and entity-relationship model of the enhanced system?

Fanciful as this dialog may seem, I believe that it implies nothing beyond current technology.   You will note that a human professional has to make judgments about the uniqueness and "unchangingness" of keys, because that depends on a knowledge of the business context and likely future.   It has notoriously been hard to teach machines enough about context for them to do good work at translating natural languages.   Requirements parsing can be seen as translating English into machine language, and it shares all of the problems of natural language translation.

Also, a human has to make judgments about the goodness of screen and report layouts.   Although there is great scope for expert systems to suggest good layouts to the analyst, the final acceptance must rest with the people who will use the display.

Now the question is, how do we get there from here?

11.2   How much expertise can be built into automated aids?

In general terms, any set of rules or procedures can be built into an expert system, and any facts that can be stored in machine-readable form can be accessed by those rules.   The difficulty in automating expertise comes in expressing human understanding in terms that can be made feasibly machine-processable.   Three factors come into play: the definability of the rules and facts, the size of the knowledge-base involved, and the computing resources needed to access it in a useful way.

Definability

Frequently, the problem turns on pinning down the exact definitions of otherwise undefined adjectives.   A human being can answer the question "Is this a meaningful name?"   An expert system has a much harder time, because it's hard to express the definition of "meaningful" in terms that a machine can use.   A human, in making such a judgment, draws on many years of education, reading, and familiarity with the business context, and even then may not be able to decide without testing the name on other humans.

Similarly, what is a "good" screen layout?   While some relatively trivial rules can be laid down (like having data areas aligned vertically), the human response to an interface remains hard to objectify.

Size of knowledge-base

A second issue is whether the expertise can be applied by using rules which operate very locally, or whether the rule, though quite definable, needs an extensive amount of data to operate on.

Take the problem of producing correctly spelled text. It is relatively simple to ensure that only letters, numbers, and valid characters like '?' are accepted. Locally enforceable rules such as "Only 'u' is permitted after 'q'" can also be implemented by simple logic. But to go beyond that, the software needs a list of allowable words (such as most spelling checkers provide); building such a list can be a non-trivial task, especially in a field like computing, with hundreds of special terms, acronyms, and abbreviations.

Computing feasibility

Even when the rules and knowledge-base are defined, the computing resources needed to implement them in a useful way may not be available or cost-effective. Ideally, each time a writer hits the space-bar after a character in a document, signifying the end of a word, the software should determine whether the word just completed is on the eligible list, and if not, lock the keyboard and sound a tone to draw the writer's attention to the putative spelling error. However, if this dictionary look-up slows down the acceptance of later characters in an annoying way, most writers would turn the facility off or find that they have acquired more shelfware. If we allow for the writer to be typing at 100 words per minute, or roughly 10 characters per second, checking a new word against the list should probably not take much more than 1/5 second if it is to be acceptable. Such performance has not been available on PCs up till now, though it may be feasible with large 386-based machines that can hold a dictionary in memory. Currently available spelling checkers typically operate as "back-end crunchers," processing a completed document and generating error messages.

What I would really value, though it would be even more demanding on computing power, would be a real-time correction suggestion facility. Suppose my word-processing system keeps track of the errors that I make, and the correct words that I substitute for them. It could be valuable for it to consult my personal "error-correction table" whenever it detects an error, and if the incorrectly spelled word is in the table, to say "Wrong: do you mean ....?" To accept the suggestions, I might hit the 'Enter' key, and then go on typing.

If it fails to find a correction in my personal table, the software could compute possible transformations of the incorrect word, removing letters, inserting letters, and considering transpositions of letters near one another on the keyboard, to see if it could figure out the word that I meant to type.   So if I entered "analyxe," the software would remove one letter at a time to see if doing so would produce a legal word, then insert each letter of the alphabet at each position in turn, then try substituting 'q', 'w', 's', and 'z' for the first 'a' and so on.   Eventually it would substitute 'z' for the 'x' and say to me "Do you mean 'analyze'?"

Consider,   however,   the very considerable number of computing cycles involved in doing this, and the MIPS needed to do it with sub-second response time.   *It is clearly possible to imagine expert assistant systems that are not (yet) feasible.*   Even if rapid error-correction of this kind were feasible, it would not catch the "legal but wrong" words, such as when "better then ever" is typed instead of "better than ever."   "Then" is an eligible word; it's just wrong in the context.   Detecting errors of this nature requires a still more extensive knowledge-base, and one that is harder to define.

Given these caveats, however, we can identify many areas in which valuable automated   support   could   be   given   to   analysis,   design,   and coding/maintenance with one or more expert systems functioning as assistants to the human analyst.   Some of these areas are discussed briefly here:

Expert system support for analysis

1.   Provide families of generic models for various commonly-used types of systems

Every business needs to do basic things like collecting money from its customers, paying its suppliers and employees, accounting for fixed assets, and keeping track of inventory.   While each business has special needs, at the logical model level there are many similarities between systems.   For example, if I say that I want to build an accounts receivable system, then the "expert assistant" could offer to display a generic DFD, a generic ERD, and generic data elements   describing   each   entity   such   as   CUSTOMER,   INVOICE, INVOICE_ITEM, PAYMENT.   It might then ask a series of questions such as "Do customers pay for shipping, or is it included in the price?"   "Is the price fixed on a price list,   negotiated separately for each sale,   or subject to a discount schedule?"   "What is the maximum number of items that can be handled on an invoice?"   Based on my answers to these questions, the expert assistant would modify the data structures and the business logic in the system model.   The result would give me a starting point for more detailed discussions with the users of the system.   Rather than saying to them "Let's build a system from scratch," I would be saying "Based on my understanding of the type of system you're looking for,   here is a first attempt at defining the data and processes involved."

The users might add or delete some data elements, and perhaps need to specify the detailed rules that they want to use e.g. for calculating discounts. But this would, hopefully, involve less effort than thinking through the specifications from scratch.

The process would be something like that involved in evaluating an application package and deciding how it needs to be changed, with the difference that the changes envisaged would be in the logical model, not in the physical code and data structures. (Indeed, when integrated CASE products are widely available, there will be little point in purchasing an application package; it will be interesting to see if package vendors start to sell the kind of "generic model" discussed here.

2. Provide a repository for information about competitor's information systems and plans

Organizations acquire considerable amounts of information about the activities of their competitors, by attending conferences, from press releases, from people interviewing for jobs, and other industry sources. Yet there is rarely a central point where this information can be collected in a standard form.

A facility for modelling our own business and systems could easily be adapted to modelling each competitor's business and systems instead. Aside from a portfolio of information systems, what hardware does a competitor have installed, on-order, and planned? How many programmers and analysts do they have? How do their salary scales compare with ours? What does all this mean in terms of their expenditure on information systems? What is their expenditure as a percentage of their revenues?

While all this information could be collected and processed by hand, automated assistance can get it into a standard, machine-processable form, and help strategic planners to get a picture of how we compare to the opposition. If our five competitors spend on IS in a range from 2% of their revenue to 5.5% of their revenue and if we spend 3%, that is a very significant fact for senior management to ponder.

3. Provide help in relating critical success factors or business objectives, to the relevant system objectives

Information systems are developed to help the organization achieve business objectives. Senior management can identify critical success factors (CSFs) such as "Become the low-cost producer," or "Improve customer service." Each CSF may imply several objectives for an information system. For example, a CSF of "Improve customer service" might translate to system objectives of "Provide access to account history while customer is on the phone," "Maintain computerized tracking of all shipments so that caller can be told exact location of each package," "Deliver statements on the nth of the month including all services rendered up to the close of the last business day of the preceding month," and so on.

An expert assistant could contain generic structures of CSFs and information system objectives for various types of business, and could question the user as to the relative importance of each. It could also help the user to think through the cost-value tradeoffs. For instance, the system might ask "What would be the value of delivering statements on the 5th of the month, as opposed to the 10th of the month?" and pool the views of several managers.

4.   Give real-time feedback on the syntax of model diagrams

As a diagram is being drawn, an expert assistant can advise as to whether the analyst is following the rules of the particular diagram type. The exact syntax rules to be checked, of course, depend on the nature of the diagram. For a DFD, they might include:

- warnings of improper data flows. For example, if the analyst tries to set up a data flow from one external entity to another, the system might display a warning and say, "You are showing a data flow between two entities which are outside your system. If this flow is truly part of the system, it must go into or out of a process. If it is not part of the system, then it should not be shown."

- checking whether object descriptions are well-formed. For example, when the analyst enters a process description, the expert assistant could verify that the first word is on the approved list of action verbs (Process, Update, Create, Compute, and so on), and if not, warn the analyst and ask whether the new verb should be added to the list.

To take another example, if name contains an external entity SYSTEM, (e.g. PAYROLL SYSTEM), the expert assistant could verify that such a system exists. The analyst could call for a pop-up window of known system names to help him name a system correctly.

Likewise, when the analyst names a data store, the assistant could verify that the data store name is a defined entity, or get the user to confirm that it should be added to the data model, and flagged for later detailed definition. When the analyst asks for a syntax check, or tries to end the session, the expert assistant could print out any free-floating objects (with no inflows or outflows) or any objects with no inflows ("magic boxes") or with no outflows ("black holes").

If the analyst does not resolve these problems immediately, the expert assistant would create a message to be displayed the next time the analyst logs on: "Discrepancies still to be resolved on Diagram No. xxx."

In this way, the diagram being created stands as good a chance as possible of being not only complete and consistent within itself, but also consistent with the ERD and with other existing system models.

5.   Help control placement of objects on diagrams and on printouts

At the most simplistic level, the software should help the analyst with the alignment of objects.   If I place a data store underneath a process, the centers of the two objects should be automatically aligned for me, as a default that I can override if I want to.

Next, the software should help with getting even distribution of objects on the diagram.   If I have many objects in one area, and only a few in other areas, I should be able to ask the expert assistant to rearrange the diagram so that objects are evenly spread out across the whole diagram area.

Most powerfully, the expert assistant could regenerate the diagram layout itself, with the aim of creating a diagram with the fewest possible line crossings, since they create visual confusion and make diagrams hard to read.

Where a diagram would spread over more than one page on a printer, the expert assistant should rearrange the diagram so that the page breaks do not cut through objects or text, but just through line connections.   In this way, the full diagram will be as readable as possible when the component pages are taped together.

6.   Given a levelled set of DFDs, produce warning where any inflows to, and outflows from, a high-level process are not shown on the lower-level explosion

Optionally, also, the expert assistant might highlight those inflows to, and outflows from, the lower-level diagram which are not shown on the higher level, so that the analyst can consider whether any of them should appear there.

Another valuable facility would be for the software to take a levelled set of diagrams, and generate a simple DFD on which all the primitive low-level processes appear.

7.   Given a description of a data element, match it with others, and name it

Suppose I am describing a data structure and need to include a data element which is concerned with the expected delivery date of a part from a supplier. Has such a data element ever been defined before in this project?   In any system in the organization?

If such a data element *does* exist (called, perhaps, EXPECTED_DELY_DTE) and I create a new one, (named, perhaps, SUPPL_PROMISE_DATE), I will have created an unnecessary synonym.   If the name has already been used, but used to mean the date when *we* expect to deliver to our customers, I risk creating a homonym (where one name means more than one thing).   My expert assistant should take the element description that I create, and match it to all the other data element descriptions (ideally in the whole organization), retrieving all the descriptions and names of those which are similar.   This will enable me to see whether I am reinventing the wheel, or whether no data element like mine has ever been defined.   In that case, the expert assistant should suggest a unique name, generated according to organizational standards.

8.   Given the source code (and data dictionary if available) for a system or systems, help to produce a logical model

This is an ambitious facility, but feasible.   Assuming that we have available the facility (discussed below) for creating an entity-relationship model from the data definitions in the various programs or in the data dictionary, the software can determine from the source code which files (tables) are read or updated by each program.   The difficulty is to determine what logical function(s) each program fulfills.   This is probably best done by the software displaying a profile of each program to the analyst, so that the analyst can give a "verb-object" name to it;   the profile would include an extract from the ERD showing the entities accessed by the program, a list of all the comments extracted from the program, images of screens used by the program, and so on.

Once the programs have been "abstracted" to logical functions in this way, the software would ask the analyst to specify what external entities provide the inputs, and what external entities receive the outputs from those programs which have to do with I/O.   Given that information, and an automatic placement algorithm, the software could draft a DFD for the analyst to review. Later in this section the issue of "reverse engineering" is considered, which means having an expert assistant to facilitate the derivation of Structured English from source code.   Such a facility would operate at a more detailed level than the one just described.

Expert system support for design

1.   Generate an ERD from database definition statements

Suppose that in a relational DBMS data dictionary, we find the two tables:

	SALES			SALES_ITEMS
K	SALE_NO		K	SALE_NO
	DATE		K	ITEM_NO
	SALESPERSON_ID			PROD_CODE
	.			QTY
	.			.
	.			.

The expert assistant can infer that there is a one-to-many relationship (or at least the potential for one) between these two tables because SALE_NO, which is the whole key of SALES, is not the whole key of SALES_ITEMS.   (It happens to be part of the key in this instance, but the argument would be the same if it were a non-key field.)   For any one value of SALE_NO in SALES, therefore, there may be more than one record with that value in SALES_ITEMS. The software can therefore create two blocks on an ERD and set up an association between them:

What the expert assistant cannot tell is the nature of the association ("contains/is part of"),   unless that is held in a comments field in a table description.   Likewise, with most current relational DBMSs, it cannot know the referential integrity constraints (whether it is allowable to have a sale without any sales items, or vice versa).   The expert assistant could ask the analyst to answer questions about referential integrity and store the answers in the ERD.

2.   Generate a physical database design from a data model,   given volumes and predicted data accesses

This, of course,   provides the converse of the facility just described.   If we know the entities, the keys and the attributes of each one, and the expected size and growth rate of the database, and the number of updates and retrievals using various fields, then an expert assistant can generate database definition statements for a given DBMS.

3.   Help with normalization of data structures.

Given a data structure, an expert assistant can query the analyst as to which element(s) uniquely identify any instance of the data structure.   If the key is a concatenated one, the software can ask "Do any of the non-key fields depend on only a part of the key?"   If so, the analyst would point to the appropriate elements, and the software would then remove them from the data structure and put them in a new data structure, in a window on the screen.   (See Chapter 5 for an example of the process.)   If the expert assistant knows of any dependencies among non-key elements, it would flag them, and ask the analyst if there were any others.

This process would be repeated until all the relevant data structures had been normalized.   The expert assistant would then display structures that had identical keys, and ask the analyst whether they should be combined.   The expert assistant would also flag data structures that had the same contents but different names, and then ask the analyst whether the names should be rationalized.

4.   Given a data structure, suggest a screen layout

Suppose you wanted to make a data entry/query screen for this data structure:

	Length
FIRST_NAME	10
MI	1
LAST_NAME	15
CITY	15
AREA_CODE	3
PHONE	8

At a simplistic level, the software could add up the lengths of each field (52 columns), and reason that with one space between each column, it could fit the entire data structure on one row of the screen. It might display the structure left-aligned, with the field names over each column as prompts:

```
FIRST_NAME M LAST_NAME       CITY            ARE PHONE
---------- - --------------- --------------- --- --------
.......... . ............... ............... ... ........
.......... . ............... ............... ... ........
```

(This is the approach taken by SQL*FORMS, discussed in Chapter 7.)

With a little more intelligence, the screen formatter could allocate the 28 spare columns equally between the six fields, so that the fields would be spaced roughly evenly across the screen, and convert the field names to upper and lower case, with spaces instead of underlines:

```
First name      M    Last name           City               Are     Phone
----------      -    ---------------     ---------------     ---     ------
..........      .    ...............     ...............     ...     ......
..........      .    ...............     ...............     ...     ......
```

If the expert assistant knows that FIRST_NAME, MI, and LAST_NAME belong together in a sub-structure, as do AREA_CODE and PHONE, they could be grouped together.

Suppose the data structure has more characters than will fit on a line?   For example, suppose we want to add STREET (20), STATE (2), and ZIP (5) to the structure above.   The expert assistant might look in the actual database and see that FIRST_NAME,   though specified as having a maximum of 10 characters,   only exceeds 8 characters in 2% of the actual records, and so on. So it might suggest a screen layout where FIRST_NAME,   LAST_NAME, STREET,   and CITY are truncated to a length which will hold 98% of the values; these fields would be programmed as scrolling areas,   so that entering "Philadelphia" in a CITY field truncated to 10 characters would end up with a display of "iladelphia" (although the whole name would be captured):

```
First     M Last name  Street               City        St Zip   Are Phone
--------  - ---------- ------------------   ----------  -- -----  --- -----
........  . .......... ..................   ..........  .. .....  .../.....
istopher  A arcantonio ighway 485 at Main  iladelphia  PA 19010  215/24588
John....  Q Public.... 1 Main Street        Anytown     OH 89222  612/58535
........  . .......... ..................   ..........  .. .....  .../.....
```

John Q. Public's details are captured in full; Christopher A. Marcantonio gets his first name, last name, street and city truncated (even though the actual data values are captured in full).

As an alternate to this layout, the expert assistant might try to split the record over two lines, placing the prompts beside their fields:

```
First name:_____ Mi:_ Last name:_____
Street:_____ City:_____ St:__ Zip:_____
```

When it finds it cannot fit all the fields on two lines, it might suggest to the analyst that it should shorten "State" to "St," change the AREA_CODE prompt to 'Phone', remove the PHONE prompt and put the phone number on the first line, aligning data areas where possible:

```
First name:_____ Mi:_ Last name:_____ Phone:___ __
   Street:_____ City:_____ St:__  Zip:_____
```

The expert assistant might display both this layout, and the one at the top of the page, with values of extreme length filled in, and ask the analyst to choose. (The analyst, of course, can always change the layouts with normal screen painting facilities.)

As well as suggesting layouts, the expert assistant would take care that installation standards for screen layout were implemented. It would also know the screen sizes and characteristics of the various CRTs to be handled, and adjust its recommendations accordingly.

5. Tell whether a screen/report is similar to any other in the system

Perhaps even before generating suggested layouts from a given data structure, as described above, the expert assistant should look at all the screens already defined in the system/organization and see whether any of them use the same data elements as the given data structure. If so, that screen should be displayed as an alternative. Clearly, if a screen has already been defined, and is in use, it is probably acceptable to the users, and other things being equal, it is better to have the same data structure displayed in the same way wherever it occurs.

Similarly, before trying to lay out a report, the analyst might name the data structure(s) to be included, and have the expert assistant display any existing reports that already use that structure(s).

Given this capability, much input/output design work can be reduced to modifying something that already exists rather than creating something from scratch.

Of course, not only the actual layout, but all the associated processing logic would potentially be inherited once the expert assistant discovered a similar screen. For instance, suppose another system already contained the logic for verifying that STATE, ZIP, and AREA_CODE all matched one another, the expert assistant would advise the analyst that this code was available for inclusion in the new system.

Expert system support for coding/maintenance

1.   **Generate code for any target language/environment from data definitions, and screen/report layouts, and process logic**

This is the function provided by the available code generator products. Clearly, once the data structures to be used have been defined, the input/output formats have been specified, and the logic to be used has been specified in some unambiguous form (such as an action diagram), the creation of code is a relatively mechanical process.   Given the appropriate generators, software can be produced in any target language, either for later compilation (as APS, TELON and IEF produce COBOL) or directly in machine language (as CorVision produces MACRO-32 code).

There is no theoretical reason, if code can be generated in one language/environment (say COBOL for CICS), why it cannot be generated in any other language/environment.   The available products limit themselves each to a relatively small group of targets, but that may well change if the market demands it.   We are thus seeing the emergence of a variety of proprietary languages, at a higher level than COBOL or PL/1 or C or ADA, which can be turned into executable code at the press of an "Enter" key.   I suggest that they be given the generic name System Development/Maintenance Languages (SDMLs).

SDMLs are partly visual in the sense that painting a screen is effectively an SDML statement, as is drawing an ERD.   They are also partly textual, in the sense that Structured English statements in an action diagram like:

```
IF SALE_TOTAL (a screen-field) GT 100
THEN DO COMPUTE_DISCOUNT
     SUBTRACT DISCOUNT FROM SALE_TOTAL
```

are textual statements.

Ideally, of course, a common standard for an SDML would emerge, but that does not seem likely, absent an initiative by IBM or the Federal Government, or by a vendor which comes to dominate the CASE field in the way that Lotus came to dominate the spreadsheet field.   Most likely, there will be a variety of dialects of SDML, distinguished by the quality and helpfulness of the expert assistants behind them.

Additionally, an expert assistant driving a generator might help the analyst to optimize the generated code either for real memory size (by using its knowledge of the functions of the various parts of the program to segment the program as efficiently as possible), or to optimize it for speed of execution.

2.   Given a program in any language, generate the corresponding SDML statements

Assuming that the expert assistant knows the structure of the database that is being accessed (as described earlier), it has to scan the program code and extract the underlying logic.   In some cases this is relatively simple;   the function of a paragraph consisting only of OPEN statements is clear.   Modules which access the database are usually fairly easy to decipher, as are modules which directly implement business logic, such as computing discounts and so on.   Of course, some code can be very obscure; if a programmer has written his own Shell sort to sequence a large table in memory, it may not be possible for even a very expert system to figure out what the purpose of the code is. One strategy at this point is for the expert assistant to display the module in question to the analyst and ask for the human to state its function.

This kind of "reverse engineering" expert assistant is somewhat similar to the COBOL restructuring tools that have been gaining popularity recently, the best known of which is probably RECODER (from Language Technology inc., Salem, MA).

In a recent study by the Federal Software Management Support Center (reported in the January 1988 issue of Software Maintenance News), RECODER was shown to help in reducing the time needed to make changes in some COBOL programs.   The most dramatic example reported was an 8000-line program, which before restructuring required 8 hours to make a change. After running the program through RECODER, the same change required only 3 hours.

However, RECODER and other restructuring tools only generate (albeit more changeable) COBOL programs, not SDML statements.   What we ultimately want is to be able to convert the existing inventory of COBOL and other programs into SDML, so that both maintenance and new development can be done at the SDML level, not the COBOL level.   This is the objective of Bachman Information Systems' Programming Assistant product.

3.   Construct database queries from English

The SDML facility would allow quite non-procedural statements to be made when access to the database is required.   The analyst might write:

```
COUNT CUSTOMERS IN MA
```

and the SDML would know enough to generate this SQL statement (assuming a relational DBMS):

```
SELECT COUNT(*) FROM CUST_TABLE
          WHERE STATE_CODE = 'MA';
```

Such a facility could be extended to allow non-technical users to pose a wide range of English-like queries, whether or not they knew the SDML syntax.   For example, a user might ask:

"Tell me how many clients we have in New England."

Using this table of synonyms:

Tell me	null
How many	COUNT
Client	CUSTOMER
We have	null
New England	MA, NH, VT, RI, ME

the query would reduce to:

COUNT CUSTOMERS IN MA, NH, VT, RI, ME.

If "New England" does not appear in the synonym table, the query software would say "Please explain what you mean by New England" and add the reply to the synonym table for later use.

It is easy in this way to construct a shallow English-like query facility, which looks intelligent provided the structure of the query remains simple.   It is harder to build in the necessary expertise to handle the query:

"How many of our customers in New England have customers in New York?"

in an intelligent way, if the concept of our customers having customers of their own has not been anticipated.   Many English query systems either will respond "I don't understand the question" or will generate:

COUNT CUSTOMERS IN MA, NH, VT, RI, ME, NY

which, of course, is quite wrong, and looks very stupid to the user.

If the expert assistant knows the structure of the database, it can respond to questions like "What data can I ask questions about?" and advise the user on the probable cost of executing a query, before it is actually submitted.

11.3 Short-to-medium-term trends

Trend #1. Toward greater integration

A review of the Vendor Direction sections in the Product Summaries will show that many of the vendors are planning to develop products that integrate modelling with code generation more closely. Vendors of modelling tools are building bridges to code generators, or improving those they already have. Vendors of code generators are building bridges to import model definitions, or grafting graphics front-ends onto their products, or adding reverse engineering capability. Vendors of products that are already integrated are seeking to widen the range of their target languages/environments.

Trend #2. Toward greater built-in expertise, available in real time

Most existing CASE products operate somewhat like word processors; they passively accept whatever is entered, store it, and regurgitate it in different forms on demand, without giving any feedback as to whether the words are correctly spelt, or the sentences are grammatical, or cliche-ridden. Where many CASE products contain built-in expertise, it is inside a "back-end cruncher," a piece of software that takes the diagrams and data definitions and generates a series of reports indicating errors, omissions, and inconsistencies.

As the discussion in Section 11.2 indicates, there is great scope for the development of expert assistant facilities which guide and warn the analyst/designer as errors and inconsistencies arise, much like an on-line spelling checker would do.

As the power of PS/2s and 32-bit workstations becomes more widely distributed, the on-line assistants will rapidly become feasible and widespread. IEW already offers on-line diagram syntax and consistency-checking on a 4Mb AT. Bachman offers on-line database design advice on a 10Mb PS/2. The latest Sun workstation (4/260) offers 10 MIPS and up to 128 Mb on your desk.

By the end of 1989, we can expect to see integrated expert assistant families that take advantage of this incredible level of power.

Trend #3. Toward larger models shared by more analysts

Several of the expert assistants suggested in Section 11.2 become most valuable when they have knowledge of all the systems in an organization, not just the immediate project. Consider how useful it would be for an analyst to be able to name a data structure, and be presented with a set of windows, one for each of the screens which displays that data structure in each of the systems in the entire firm.   Provided security is not compromised, it would seem to be productive to have a single model of all the organization's information systems, accessible by everyone who needs to do so.   The increase in desktop power and the availability of high-speed networks will make this feasible.

Trend #4.   Toward a visual/textual modelling language that describes all systems

If a diagram, built up interactively with an automated expert assistant, can be automatically turned into database definition statements, then which is the actual language used, the diagram or the DDL?

If the statement "COUNT CUSTOMERS IN NEW ENGLAND" can be automatically converted to

```
SELECT COUNT(*) FROM CUST_TABLE
   WHERE STATE_CODE IN ('MA', 'NH', 'VT', 'RI', 'ME')
```

which is embedded in a COBOL program which is compiled to machine language,   then which is the actual language used,   the System Development/Maintenance Language (SDML) or COBOL?

The test, of course, must be "which language is changed by the maintenance programmer in the middle of the night?"

If the DDL and COBOL can be hidden (or not generated), so that maintenance must be done on the SDML, and the developers/maintainers can still do everything they want to do in SDML, then COBOL will finally have been made obsolete.

As we noted in Section 11.2, an SDML will be partly visual, partly textual. Once reverse-engineering facilities are available,   it will be feasible for organizations to translate their existing code and data definitions into SDML, where they can be rationalized, and regenerated in COBOL, or C, or directly into machine-language.

Part II

A detailed analysis of EXCELERATOR

This part consists of a fairly detailed description of the most widely available CASE product, EXCELERATOR, developed and marketed by Index Technology.

Although EXCELERATOR falls short of being an ideal product, lacking a process description language and tight integration with a code-generation facility, it is nevertheless an outstandingly well-designed, well-supported, and successful product.

Close examination of its facilities is recommended, not least as a basis for comparison with other products.

EXCELERATOR

EXCELERATOR is a PC-based product, with extensive graphical modelling capability, using semantic color, integrated with a repository stored on the PC disk. Graphical symbols and syntax can be user-modified with an extra-charge upgrade. Screen and report layouts can be prototyped and execution simulated to a limited extent. Screen layouts and data definitions can be exported to several code-generators marketed by other firms (e.g. Pansophic's TELON). Extensive project management support is also available.

Runs on: XT/AT/VAX/SUN/Apollo **Vendor:** Index Technology
                      1 Main St
Min. config: 640K, 10Mb, mouse, EGA   Cambridge MA 02142
Price: $8400 for first copy   617/494-8200

Also markets EXCELERATOR/RTS for modelling real time systems and PC/PRISM for planning.

GRAPHICS: Described later in this Part.

REPOSITORY: Described later in this Part.

PROTOTYPING: Described later in this Part.

CODE GENERATION: Described later in this Part.

DOCUMENT GENERATION: Described later in this Part.

PROJECT MANAGEMENT SUPPORT: Work breakdown structure diagram. Dictionary entities mapped to project, task. Direct integration with ABTs Project Manager Workbench. Interfaces to other PM packages.

DESIGN ASSISTANCE: Described later in this Part.

OTHER FEATURES: AFIPS Software Product of the Year 1987. Index Tech was the first front-end CASE vendor to have a public stock offering.

VENDOR DIRECTION: Support entire development process.
Provide rigorous support for variety of methodologies, eg IDEF.
Facilitate use of reusable system definition components.
Enhance graphics interface using emerging industry standards for windowing. Support OS2/PM and X-Windows.
Provide additional interfaces to a variety of other software products.
Expand support for two-way communication of data from and to the Repository so that it can be kept synchronized with the physical system. Enhance the structure of the Repository.
Provide enhanced networking and multi-user access.
Interface to IBM Repository; SAA compatibility.

EXCELERATOR

Main Menu

When you invoke EXCELERATOR, you are asked for your user ID and password. Once these are entered correctly, you are shown a list of the projects which you can access. Once you select a project, EXCELERATOR displays its main menu, which gives you the choices:

Selecting this choice . . .	Allows you to . . .
GRAPHICS	. . . draw ■ data flow diagrams ■ entity-relationship/ data model diagrams ■ structure charts/structure diagrams ■ presentation graphs (IBM flowchart symbols plus some others) See Section 2, Graphics
XLDICTIONARY	. . . update the Repository directly, and list its current contents. See Section 3, Repository.
SCREENS & REPORTS	. . . build up screen and report layouts, and simulate screen data entry. See Section 4, Prototyping.
DOCUMENTATION	. . . assemble and print e.g. a specification document, pulling together diagrams (developed with the graphics facility), Repository entries, screen/report layouts, and narrative documents from external word processors (e.g. WORD). See Section 6, Document Generation.
ANALYSIS	. . . produce reports that evaluate diagrams, list entries in the Repository, and analyze the completeness and consistency of the Repository contents. See Section 3, Repository.
XLD INTERFACE	. . . export some or all of the Repository to a transfer file, import data, lock data to restrict access by others, and unlock so that other analysts can share your work. See Section 3, Repository, and Section 5, Code Generation.
HOUSEKEEPING	. . . set up new projects, do backup/restore, change passwords and other access facilities, make printer/plotter selection, set diagram defaults (e.g. font size), and set other project parameters.

EXCELERATOR

Drawing diagrams

To draw a diagram, select the Graphics option from the Main Menu. The alternatives displayed then are

Data Flow Diagram   A suitably authorized user (usually the Project Manager) can select whether Gane/Sarson or Yourdon conventions are used.

Structure Chart

Data Model Diagram

Entity/Relationship Diagram   The Project Manager can select whether Chen or Merise conventions are used.

Structure Diagram

Presentation Graph

Once you select a diagram type, you can select the specific diagram you want to work on from a list, or enter its name. You can also choose to Modify, Delete, Copy, Rename, or List the diagram that you select, or Add a new diagram.

Each type of diagram has its own menu of objects (e.g. PROCESS) that you can select to draw, and its menu of operations (e.g. CONNECT two objects). The menu is displayed in the left margin, as shown in this sample Gane/Sarson data flow diagram screen:*

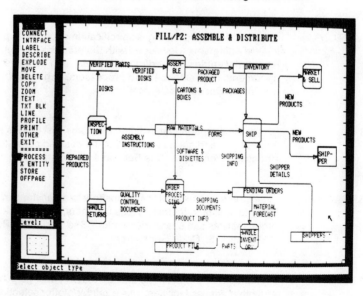

The small rectangular area in the bottom left corner of the screen is the Orientation Map; this shows a dot for every object in the diagram.

*   The diagrams in this section are reproduced by kind permission of Index Technology Corp:

132

Drawing diagrams (cont'd)

To add an object

Select OBJECT from the graphics menu, then select the type of object (e.g. PROCESS on a Data Flow Diagram, FUNCTION on a Structure Chart, etc.). Place the cursor where you want the object to appear; it will be centered at the intersection of the nearest grid lines (the marks along the edges of the drawing area). The grid spacing can be set to one of six spacings: No Grid, Fine, Small, Medium (the default), Large, or Coarse. Examples of the resulting object spacing are:

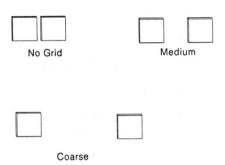

No Grid   Medium

Coarse

When an object is first added to a diagram, it has no name or identifier (ID). To give it a name, select LABEL from the graphics menu, then type in the name (e.g. CUSTOMERS for an external entity, MAINTAIN CURRENT PRODUCT INVENTORY for a Process, etc.), up to 60 characters. When you view the object in Close Up Zoom (see Viewing Diagrams below), you will see the whole label. If you view it in Medium or Layout zoom, the label will be displayed according to the setting of Label Mode, previously established with the Profile command (part of HOUSEKEEPING). Typical effects of the various Label Modes are:

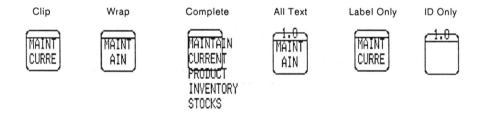

The number of characters shown also depends on font and object size.

Connections can be labelled; if you choose the SysLabel option, EXCELERATOR will place the label according to its own logic, typically above a horizontal connection and to the right of a vertical one. You can move SysLabels if you don't like their position.

EXCELERATOR

Drawing diagrams (cont'd)

If you choose UsrLabel, you can create a window for your label by selecting the upper left and lower right corners of an area.   However, if you then move the connection, your UsrLabel will stay where you put it; you have to move it in a separate operation.

An object doesn't have an ID until you have described it to the Repository.   (See Interfacing a Diagram... below.)

To connect two objects

Select CONNECT from the menu, then decide whether you want to choose the path for the connection line or let EXCELERATOR do it for you.   If you want to choose the path yourself, select the object from which the connection is to start, then select each bend point, then finally the object on which the connection is to end.   If you want EXCELERATOR to do its best to choose a path, using its built-in logic, just select the two objects.

The path chosen will depend on settings previously established with the Profile command.   If you choose Pipe as opposed to Straight, the connections will be drawn horizontally and vertically with rounded bends.   If you choose Straight, you will get straight lines.   If you choose One Way connections, you will get an arrowhead at the second object; if you choose Two Way or No Arrow, you will get two arrowheads or none, as shown here:

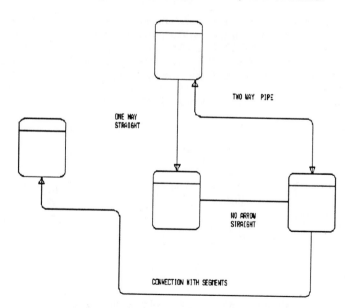

You can specify the exact point of attachment of a connection to an object (the "port") if you choose the Userport option (again with the Profile command).   If you choose Systport (the default), EXCELERATOR will select the ports based on its built-in logic.

Drawing diagrams (cont'd)

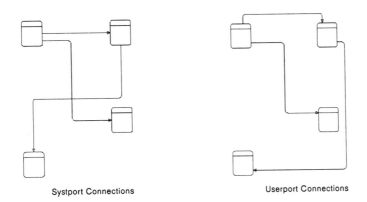

Systport Connections   Userport Connections

Each graph object has 24 possible ports. The locations of the ports can be changed using the CUSTOMIZER facility.

To move an object

Select MOVE from the menu, then select the object that you want to move, then select the location to which you want to move it. The object's label and any connections are moved with it. EXCELERATOR will redraw the diagram; if you have specified SaveConn (part of Profile), EXCELERATOR will keep the original ports and bend points. If you chose ChgConn, EXCELERATOR will redraw the correction.

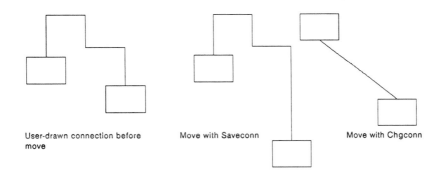

User-drawn connection before move   Move with Saveconn   Move with Chgconn

With a Structure Chart, Structure Diagram, or Document Graph, you can choose the Profile setting MoveHry (Move Hierarchy). Then if you move an object, all objects below it in the hierarchy are moved with it so as to keep the same sub-structure. If you choose Move One, only the selected object is moved.

EXCELERATOR

Drawing diagrams (cont'd)

To move a connection (e.g. to minimize the crossing of lines), select the end of the connection that you want to move, select a new location for the end, and then (optionally) select new bend-points.

To undo a change

When you are drawing a path for a connection, you can press Cancel and undo the last part of the line that you just drew. Other than that, EXCELERATOR has no explicit Undo; if you don't like the result of a Move, say, you have to do another Move to get the drawing back the way it was. (Of course, you can save a diagram before making a change, and then simply reload the saved version if you want to undo the change.)

To align one object with another

Since objects are centered on grid intersections, alignment is automatic.

Viewing and printing diagrams

To see the whole diagram

Select ZOOM from the graphics menu, and select LAYOUT from the options menu (below the main menu). The whole diagram will be shown, though of course the labels may be hard to read. As an example:

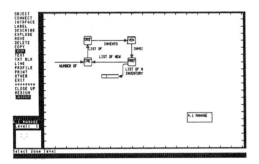

To see part of a diagram close up

EXCELERATOR has only two levels of magnification, MEDIUM and CLOSE UP, as shown here:

Medium   **Close up**

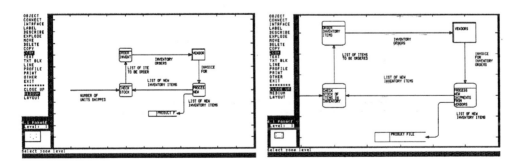

In CLOSE UP, the complete text of all labels is displayed; it may be truncated at other levels.

EXCELERATOR

Viewing and printing diagrams (cont'd)

To select an area that you want magnified, select a point on the diagram, either on the orientation map or on the drawing screen. That point will become the center of the new display. If you are at MEDIUM or CLOSE UP and you don't change the level, the effect will be to pan (move the window) across the diagram.

To print a diagram

If you select PRINT and the DRAFT option, you can print a draft of the diagram which has the whole diagram, no matter how large, on one sheet of the printer's paper. While a DRAFT print-out shows the general layout, the labels may be truncated.

To print all or part of a diagram in full detail, select the FULL GPH or WINDOW options, respectively. (EXCELERATOR refers to a diagram as a graph.) You can select the actual size that you want the objects to print out at, and you can select the font size to be used for labels, (provided your printer can print that font).

When you select FULL GPH, then if the printed diagram will spread over more than one page, EXCELERATOR shows you where the page breaks will come, like this:

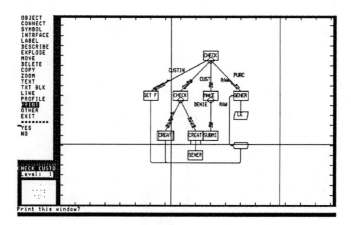

This gives you a chance to adjust the diagram layout to fit on the minimum number of pages or have the page breaks at the least inconvenient points.

Diagrams can be stored in a file for printing later, if required.

Interfacing with the Repository

To put the description of an object into the Repository

When you first draw a diagram, the objects and connections (entities) are stored as images, with no corresponding entries in the Repository (called XLDICTIONARY in EXCELERATOR). You have to explicitly describe each entity to build the Repository. To do so, select DESCRIBE from the graphics menu, then select the entity you want to describe. EXCELERATOR will present you with the right type of description screen for that entity.

To describe a data store, EXCELERATOR gives you a screen like this:

To describe a process, EXCELERATOR gives you a screen like this:

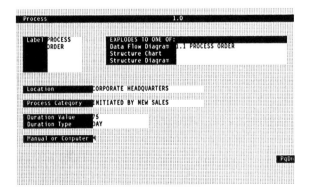

Each entity (object or connection) must be given an ID (on the top line of the screen) which is unique within its entity type. Thus there can only be one data store with an ID of 1.0, and there can only be one process with an ID of 1.0. Labels, on the other hand, need not be unique.

EXCELERATOR

Interfacing with the Repository (cont'd)

Note that each entity can be exploded to other entities, which hold more detail. In the example on the previous page, the detailed contents of Data Store 1.0 - CUSTOMER FILE will be found in Data Record 2.0. For full details of these explosions, see Section 3 on the Repository.

To see/specify the contents/explosion of an object

Provided you (or someone on your project) has described the lower-level entity which a given entity explodes to, you can select EXPLODE from the graphics menu and then select the entity you are interested in. EXCELERATOR will display the more detailed diagram or screen. For instance, if you explode the data store INVOICES, you might get a screen like this, describing the structure of the Record INVOICE:

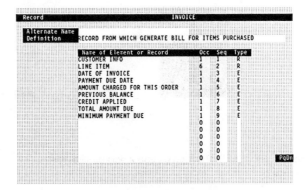

(For an explanation of Occ, Seq, and Type, see Section 3.)

If you have described a process on a data flow diagram as exploding to a lower level data flow diagram, then that detailed diagram will be displayed.

EXCELERATOR allows unlimited levels of diagram explosion.

Graphics limitations

1. The number of objects on a diagram is limited by main memory to some 75 objects on a 640K RAM machine. Larger platforms do not have this limitation.

2. It can be inconvenient to have only three levels of magnification, especially since labels are truncated, except in CLOSE UP mode.

Repository

The EXCELERATOR Repository (called the XLDICTIONARY) is implemented with a C-tree data base on the disk of the PC or other platform, maintaining its own indexes.

Repository structure

The main entities and relationships stored are shown in this diagram:

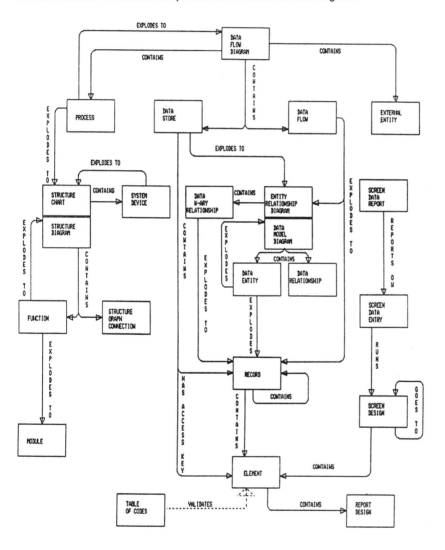

This diagram is to be read (e.g. at the top) as saying that a DATA FLOW DIAGRAM may contain a PROCESS, a PROCESS may explode to a DATA FLOW DIAGRAM, and so on.

EXCELERATOR

Brief descriptions of each entity supported by EXCELERATOR
(in order of abbreviation):

DAE	Data Entity	A group of (one or more) data ELEs on a DMD or ERA.
DAF	Data Flow	A group of ELEs moving along an arrow on a DFD.
DAR	Data Relationship	An association between two or more DAEs.
DAS	Data Store	A place on a DFD where data is stored.
DCG	Document Graph	An outline of a document produced within EXCELERATOR.
DFD	Data Flow Diagram	A logical model of a system showing the relationships between the PRCs, the DASs, the EXTs, and the DAFs that carry data into, around, and out of the system.
DMD	Data Model Diagram	A picture of a data structure showing the DARS between DAEs.
DNR	Data N-ary Relationship	An association showing multiple dependencies between DAEs on an ERA.
DOF	Document Fragment	The smallest component of a DCG.
DOC	Document Group	A collection of DOFs that share a common title.
ELE	Element	The smallest unit of data within a REC.
ELS	Entity List	A user-created subset of entities.
ERA	Entity-Relationship Diagram	A picture of a data structure showing the DARS between DAEs. (Note that the standard abbreviation is ERD.)
EXT	External Entity	A source or destination of data on a DFD.
FUN	Function	A procedure which implements a PRC, with one or more MODs.
MOD	Module	A unit of software that carries out a FUN.
PGC	Presentation Graph Connection	A relationship between two or more objects on a PRG.
PGO	Presentation Graph Object	Any of the objects on a PRG.

PRC   Process

An object on a DFD; a set of operations that transforms incoming DAFs into outgoing DAFs.

PRG   Presentation Graph

A free-form diagram used for flow-charting, decomposition diagrams, and other presentations.

REC   Record

A named group of ELEs or other RECs, treated as a unit.

RED   Report Design

A summary screen for a prototype system report layout.

REP   Report

A summary screen for a report analyzing the contents of the Repository.

SCD   Screen Design

A summary screen for a prototype screen layout.

SDE   Screen Data Entry

A summary screen for exercising a SCD by entering data.

SDR   Screen Data Report

A summary screen for a report analyzing a file created via SDE.

SDV   System Device

An object on a STC standing for any I/O device, or the environment (e.g. the operating system).

SGC   Structure Graph Connection

The flow of data/control between two FUNs on a STC or STD.

STC   Structure Chart

A picture of the invocation hierarchy of FUNs within a PRC (Constantine notation).

STD   Structure Diagram

A picture of the invocation hierarchy of FUNs within a PRC (Jackson notation).

TAB   Table of Codes

User-defined codes and meanings used for field validation.

USR   User

A person, group, etc with responsibilities in the target system.

EXCELERATOR

What is held about a data element?

ID (name)
Alternate names (3)
Definition   Displays as a Help message when the element is used in screen design.
Input picture   }   Used when the element is included as a field in a screen
                         }   design.
Output picture   }
Edit rules   }   Can be a range, or in terms of a named table of values
Storage type   C - character, B - binary, P - packed, F - floating pt., D - date
Characters left of decimal
Characters right of decimal
Prompt
Column header   }   For reports.
Short header   }
Base or derived   A base element is not derived by any process in the system; e.g. it is captured by data entry.

Data class
Source
Default   Value which the element should default to on a screen.
Description   Up to 60 lines of 72 characters.

What is held about a data store?

ID (name)
Label   As on the DFD(s) that include the data store.
Explodes to: Data Record, Data Model Diagram, or E-R Diagram.
Location   Where the data store is/will be physically located.
Manual or Computer   M or C
Number of records   Maximum expected.
Index elements   Data elements within the detailed record which may be used as search arguments for access.
Description   Up to 60 lines of 72 characters.

The detailed contents of a data store is held in one or more Records to which the Data Store is exploded. Each Record in turn may include up to 115 sub-Records, or Elements, as shown on the next page:

What is held about a data store? (cont'd)

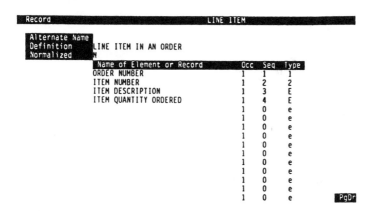

CUSTOMER INFO occurs once in INVOICE and is itself a Record (Type is R), as is LINE ITEM, which occurs up to six times. To list all the elements that make up CUSTOMER INFO, each of these component Records would also have to be exploded.

Type R is a record; Type E is an Element. Type K means an Element that is the whole key identifier of the Record. If the key contains more than one Element (is concatenated), Type is a number from 1 to 9 for each such Element.

You can set the Normalized field to "Y" to signify that the Record structure is normalized and should be considered by those analysis reports which check normalized Records.

EXCELERATOR

What is held about a process?

ID (name)
Label   As on the DFD(s) that include the process.
Explodes to   Data Flow Diagram, Structure Chart, or Structure Diagram.
Location   Where the process is/will be physically located.
Process category
Duration value   If duration value is 100 and duration type is WEEK, the process
Duration type   is/will be performed 100 times a week.
Manual or Computer   M or C
Description   Up to 60 lines of 72 characters each.

Note that EXCELERATOR has no explicit facility for storing process logic; the Description field can be used to hold up to 60 lines of Structured English or Action Diagram, but all editing and alignment is your responsibility. The Description field is just text; if you use an Element name in the logic, EXCELERATOR can't connect that use to the Element definition.

How does meta-data get into the Repository?

For the entities that appear on a diagram (such as Processes, Data Entities and so on), you select DESCRIBE from the Graphics menu, select the entity on the diagram, and fill in the attributes on the entity Description screen that EXCELERATOR displays for you.

For the other entities (such as Records and Elements) that don't appear on diagrams, you can either enter meta-data about them through the Graphics facility, or call up their Description screens from the XLDICTIONARY menu, and enter the meta-data in that way.

EXCELERATOR automatically records the following audit attributes for each entity:

- the ID of the user who originally created it, and the date
- the ID of the user who last modified it, and the date
- the number of times the entity has been modified altogether
- the project in which the entity was created, or from which it has been imported
- whether the entity is currently locked (implying someone is in process of changing it), and if so:
- the ID of the user who locked it, and the date it was locked. (Entity data can be locked and unlocked as part of the XLDINTERFACE option on EXCELERATOR's main menu.)

How can Repository contents be accessed/analyzed?

Access Privileges

Each user on a given project is assigned an access privilege, normally by the Project Manager:
READ users can see the Repository meta-data but cannot change it.
LIMITED users can see the Repository and can change and delete data, provided that no other user has locked the entity in question.
MASTER users can do anything to everything, even changing entities that other users have locked.

XLDICTIONARY Menus

When you select XLDICTIONARY from EXCELERATOR's main menu, you are given a menu of entity classes; if you make a selection from that menu, you can then select a specific entity from the 32 possibilities:

Entity classes	Entities
REC/ELE	Record (REC)
	Element (ELE)
DATA	Data Store (DAS)
	Data Entity (DAE)
	Data Flow (DAF)
	Data Relationship (DAR)
	Data N-ary Relationship (DNR)
PROCESS	Process (PRC)
	Function (FUN)
	System Device (SDV)
	External Entity (EXT)
	Module (MOD)
	Presentation Graph Object (PGO)
	Structure Graph Connection (SGC)
	Presentation Graph Connection (PGC)
GRAPHS	Data Flow Diagram (DFD)
	Data Model Diagram (DMD)
	Entity-Relationship Diagram (ERA)
	Presentation Graph (PRG)
	Structure Chart (STC)
	Structure Diagram (STD)
	Document Graph (DCG)
SCR/REP	Report Design (RED)
	Screen Design (SCD)
	Screen Data Entry (SDE)
	Screen Data Report (SDR)
OTHER	Document Group (DOC)
	Document Fragment (DOF)
	Report (REP)
	Entity List (ELS)
	User (USR)
	Table of Codes (TAB)

EXCELERATOR

From these menus, you can

1. Select the standard Description screen (e.g. for a REC), enter the entity name (e.g. INVOICE), see what is stored about it, and change the data on the screen, if you are privileged to do so.

2. Produce a standard report by selecting
    -   an entity (e.g. REC) **plus**
    -   one of the relationships in which it may be involved (e.g. REC contains ELE), **plus**
    -   either the name of a specific entity (e.g. CUSTOMER ACCOUNT), or a "name range" (e.g. "CUST*," which will give you all the RECs whose names begin with CUST); **plus**
    -   a standard output type e.g. Summary Output, as shown here:

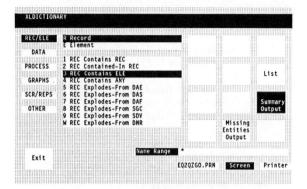

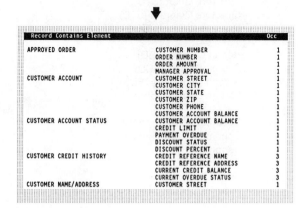

In the example above, "*" has been entered for the name range; this will result in all RECs being included in the output.

More detailed analysis can be done by selecting ANALYSIS from EXCELERATOR's main menu; EXCELERATOR will then give you four choices:

GRAPH ANALYSIS	Enables you to run one of four diagram analysis reports (see below).
ENTITY LIST	Enables you to build up a stored list of entities e.g. for exporting to another project (see below).
REPORT WRITER	Produces custom reports on multiple entity types (see next page).
EXTENDED ANALYSIS	Builds a series of matrices analyzing the current contents of the Repository, from which you can generate reports assessing completeness and consistency.

Each of these analysis options has its own sub-menus, summarized in the following pages.

GRAPH ANALYSIS has four options:

Verification Report	Lists illegal connections (e.g. between two External Entities) and freestanding objects (with no connections to other objects) on a given DFD.
Analysis Report	Summarizes inputs and outputs for each Process and Data Store on a DFD.
Level Balancing Report	Indicates whether the data flows in and out of a process on one level of a DFD are consistent with the flows on a lower explosion level.
Graph Explosion	Lists explosion paths of objects and connections (i.e. what explodes to what).

EXCELERATOR

ENTITY LIST

It is often convenient to work with a list of entities, e.g. all entities added since a given date, or everything to do with ORDERS. To create an entity list, select Add, which has eight options:

Add

Screen input

EXCELERATOR displays a screen for you to name a new list and key in the names of the entities explicitly.

Union

enables you to make a new list by combining two existing lists; entities in both lists appear only once in the new list.

Intersection

enables you to make a new list by combining two existing lists; only the entities in both lists appear in the new list to check, e.g., for duplication.

Difference

is the converse of Intersection; entities that are in both lists do not appear in the new list.

Subtraction

removes from the first list any entities in the second list.

XLD Selection

enables you to make a new list by selecting entities from the XL Dictionary by specifying selection rule(s) in terms of their attributes, e.g. all Data Stores modified in the past month.

XLD Selection from List

enables you to make a new list from an existing list by specifying a selection rule(s).

XLD Report Execution

enables you to make a new list by using selection criteria previously defined in Report Writer (see next page).

REPORT WRITER

If the standard reports available through XLDICTIONARY are not adequate, you can produce a wide variety of custom reports to help in analyzing your Repository contents:

If you select REPORT WRITER from the ANALYSIS menu, you will be given four options:

Entity List   is used to produce a report on a set of entities already defined in an entity list.

Select   is used when no suitable Entity List exists.   You can select entities from the XL Dictionary by specifying selection rule(s) in terms of their attributes, e.g. all Data Stores modified in the past month, or all Processes created by a certain analyst.

(Choose Entity List or Select, whichever is the most convenient way of specifying the entities that you want in your report.)

Sort   is used if you want the report in a particular sequence; up to nine entity attribute fields can be used.

Format   is used to specify the report layout that you want. Format options are:

    User-Defined   allows you to:

-   select which entity attributes you want to appear in the report
-   lay out the attributes in any order you want across a page of up to 132 chars
-   specify a title at the top of the report
-   modify headers for each of the columns
-   adjust the width of a column
-   delete a column from the report
-   scroll left and right among the column headers
-   count the non-blank entries in any column
-   total the values in a numeric column

    Output   Provides complete description for each entity in the report.

    Summary Output   Name and two other attributes for each entity in the report.

    List   Displays on the screen the name and one other attribute for each entity in the report. (Lists cannot be printed.)

    Audit Output   Lists the audit attributes (Date created, date last modified etc.)

    Missing Entities Output   Lists entities that you include in the report but that are not yet defined in the Repository.

EXCELERATOR

EXTENDED ANALYSIS provides six analysis programs, each of which builds one or more matrices analyzing the current contents of the Repository (doing so can take substantial amounts of machine time on a large project; e.g. processing 5 megabytes of data can take an hour or more). You can either print out the matrices directly or, more meaningfully, produce a selection from the 33 different reports summarized below and examine these reports to assess the completeness and consistency of the Repository.

The Extended Analysis menu has six options:

Record Content Analysis - 6 reports looking at potentially redundant data.

Key Validation Analysis - 8 reports looking at completeness and consistency of key data elements.

Data Model Validation Analysis - 3 reports comparing connections on each Data Model Diagram to the Data Relationships you have described in the Repository.

Data Normalization Analysis - 7 reports checking the Records that you have flagged with a 'Y' in the "Normalized" column.

Screen/Report Data Usage - 3 reports looking at the elements used in each Screen and Report Design and flagging pairs of designs that appear to use similar data.

Element Access and Derivation Analysis - 6 reports looking for ELEs which are not contained in any data flow, and looking at the validity of the Base/Derived attribute for those elements that are contained in data flows.

Each report is summarized below.

Record Content Analysis generates these reports:

Empty Records	lists Records that contain no Elements or other Records.
Recursive Records	lists Records that appear to contain themselves; e.g. if ORDERS contains ITEMS, and ITEMS is specified as containing ORDERS, there's a problem.
Equivalent Records	lists pairs of Records that when exploded down to their elements, contain the same elements.
Subset Records	lists pairs of Records where all the elements of one record are in another records, but not vice versa.
Similar Records	lists pairs of Records where each has a high percentage of elements in common with the other. You can set the cutoff percentage; the default is 75%.
Partial Subset Records	is like Similar Records, but lists pairs where many of the elements of one record are elements of the other.

Key Validation Analysis generates five matrices holding information about Record contents and Elements specified as keys and/or indexes.   Once the matrices have been built, you can run any of these reports:

Unkeyed Records (One Level) — lists Records with no keys specified directly in their contents.

Multiple Key Records (One Level) — lists any Records which appear to be specified to have more than one key

Key Elements (One Level) — lists each Element which has been specified as a (part or whole) key anywhere in the project, together with the corresponding Record.

Foreign Keys (All Levels) — lists each Element specified as a key in one Record that appears as a non-key Element in any other Record.

Inherited Keys — lists each top-level Record in the whole project, together with all key Elements specified anywhere in that Record's contents, directly or through explosion.

Unkeyed Records (All Levels) — lists top-level Records that have no key specified, either directly or through explosion.

Data Store Exceptions — lists any Data Store that does not explode to a top-level Record with a defined key.

Index Element Exceptions — lists any Data Store for which no index elements have been specified, and each Data Store whose explosion Record does not contain the Elements specified as being indexes.

Data Model Validation Analysis compares the connections on Data Model Diagrams with what you have stored in the Repository about the corresponding Data Relationships. Three reports can be produced:

Undescribed Data Relationships — lists any connections you have shown on any Data Model Diagrams but have not described as Data Relationships in the Repository, together with their associated Data Entities.

Modified Data Relationships — lists Data Relationships whose definitions have been completed by running Data Model Validation (in fact, when you run this report).

DMD/DAR Exceptions — lists conflicts between what has been drawn on Data Model Diagrams and what has been specified in the Repository.

EXCELERATOR

Data Normalization Analysis builds seven matrices, analyzing Records. Seven reports can be produced:

Repeating Groups
lists Records that contain Records and Elements that occur more than once (and so cannot be in 1NF).

Element Access Conflicts
lists non-key Elements that depend on different keys in different Records.

Matching Key Records
lists pairs of Records with identical keys, or where one Record has a key which is part of another Record's (concatenated) key.

Record Dependencies
lists Records whose key Elements are a subset of the key and/or non-key Elements in another Record.

Data Entity Exceptions
lists Data Entities that cannot be analyzed further, because they do not explode to any Record, or explode to a Record not flagged as normalized, or explode to a structural Record, or explode to a Record with repeating groups, or to one with no specified key.

Data Model Relationships
lists Records that explode from Data Entities related by Data Relationships, indicating whether these are 1:1, 1:Many, or Many:Many.

DAR/Record Conflicts
lists pairs of Records whose keys are in conflict with the descriptions of Data Relationships in Data Model Diagrams.

Screen/Report Data Usage can produce six reports:

Elements in Screen/Report Designs lists the Elements used by each Design.

Equivalent Screen/Report Designs
lists pairs of Designs that use exactly the same Elements.

Subset Screen/Report Designs
lists pairs of Designs where the Elements used in one Design are a subset of the Elements used in the other.

Element Access and Derivation Analysis

Unexploded Data Flows   lists Data Flows that do not explode to any Records.

Unprocessed Elements   lists Elements not contained in Records that explode from Data Flows.

Element Processing   lists selected Elements and the Processes that implicitly use them (because the Elements are contained in Records that explode from Data Flows that enter or leave a given Process).

Element Traceability   lists selected Elements and the path of their usage through Records, Data Flows, and Processes.

Misused Base Elements   lists Elements that you have specified as "Base" in the Repository but which are implicitly derived by some Process on some DFD (because they appear to leave the Process but do not appear to enter it).

Misused Derived Elements   lists Elements that you have specified as "Derived" in the Repository but which do not appear to be derived by any Process on any DFD.

EXCELERATOR

Prototyping

Selecting SCREENS & REPORTS from EXCELERATOR's main menu gets you these four facilities:

Report Design allows you to interactively lay out report formats on the screen (scrolling left and right to get up to 132 characters). The Output Pictures that were defined in the Repository for each Element can be inserted in a Report Design to give the lengths and types of fields.

Screen Design allows you to interactively lay out a screen with text, prompts, repeating fields/rows, and help messages. One screen can be chained to the next to be displayed. You can extract a field's length, data type, default value, and so on from the Repository, or you can define them specially for any given screen. Fields can be moved on the screen by a Cut operation (to move the field to a buffer) followed by a Paste operation.

Screen Data Entry allows you to create a file for storing data entered through a given Screen Design and then populate that file, e.g. with representative client order data or customer addresses.

Screen Data Reporting enables you to generate reports extracting data from a file populated through Screen Data Entry, sorting it and formatting it as required. (A maximum of 38 fields can be handled.)

Thus EXCELERATOR screen prototyping

CAN:
- simulate data entry.
- simulate invocation of the next screen from the bottom of the previous one.
- edit values that are entered, for data type, and for conformity to Element edit rules.

CANNOT:
- compute screen fields as data is entered, e.g. multiplying QUANTITY by UNIT_PRICE to give ITEM_TOTAL.
- simulate queries (database retrieval) and updating of existing records.
- simulate inter-field editing, e.g. checking if ORDER_TOTAL exceeds CREDIT_LIMIT.
- handle a record of more than 2047 characters.
- simulate skipping of certain fields.
- simulate transfer of control to more than one screen.

156

Code Generation

EXCELERATOR can export data structure definitions for use in COBOL, BASIC, C, and PL/I programs, and can also export ASCII files for input to a variety of code generator packages.

Screen Designs can be exported as **data maps** or as **interface files** by selecting the "Generate" option from within Screen Design.

Data maps can be merged directly into target language code. You have to specify
- a name for the map (default is the name of the Screen Design).
- a prefix to be added to all the data names in the map, to help with uniqueness (can be omitted).

As an example, here is a COBOL screen data map where the prefix specified was ORD:

```
*Record ORDER-INFO. Compiled:  2-JUL-86
 01  ORDER-INFO.
     05  ORDOrder-Number  PIC X(11).
     05  ORDDate          PIC X(8).
     05  ORDCustomer      PIC X(29).
     05  ORDAttention     PIC X(32).
     05  ORDProduct-Info. OCCURS 15 TIMES.
         10  ORDProduct-Number
                           PIC X(8).
         10  ORDQuantity  PIC XXXX.
         10  ORDUnit-Price
                           PIC X(7).
         10  ORDTotal-Price
                           PIC X(7).
     05  ORDTax           PIC X(7).
     05  ORDSubtotal      PIC X(8).
     05  ORDTotal         PIC $9999.99.
     05  ORDShipping-Address
                           OCCURS 6 TIMES.
         10  ORDShipping-Address
                           PIC X(25).
     05  ORDAddress       OCCURS 6 TIMES.
         10  ORDShiping-Address
                           PIC X(25).
     05  ORDOrder-Taken-By
                           PIC XXX.
     05  ORDMarketing-Rep.
                           PIC XXX.
     05  ORDInvoice-Number
                           PIC X(8).
```

Interface files contain the screen definition information as an ASCII file, with a format specified for each line of the file.

BMSGEN and MFSGEN, two products from The Hobbs Group (Box 02171, Portland, OR, 97202, phone 503/771-8991) enable Screen Designs to be translated into BMS maps for CICS, or MFS maps for IMS/DC.

Record structures can also be generated as Outside Products (e.g. for export to mainframe data dictionaries).
Outside Products are flat, ASCII files containing 80-character records, with a variety of formats.

EXCELERATOR

XL/Interface TELON is a separately priced enhancement to EXCELERATOR. It allows Screen and Report Designs to be smoothly converted into input for Pansophic's application generator TELON.

XL/Interface for Micro Focus Workbench is another separately priced enhancement. It allows structure charts to be converted into skeleton COBOL programs, and allows Screen and Report Designs to be converted to COBOL data descriptions. The Micro Focus COBOL Workbench (which also runs on a PC) can then be used to interactively write and test a COBOL program using the generated skeleton and data definitions.

XL/Interface TELON

This is an enhanced version of EXCELERATOR (corporate license $9,000). It allows Screen and Report Designs to be smoothly converted into input for the application generator TELON (from Pansophic Systems, 709 Enterprise Drive, Oak Brook, IL, 60521, phone 312/572-6000).

XL/Interface TELON provides a new kind of diagram in the Graphics facility called a Circle Flow Diagram, which is TELON's variant of the Dialogue Flow Diagram described in Part 1, as shown here:

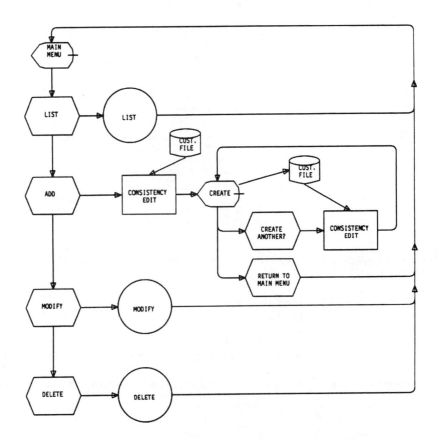

You should build up a Circle Flow Diagram for each linked group of screens in an application and describe to EXCELERATOR the flow of data and control between them. The details of each screen, of course, are specified in a Screen Design.

Screens and Reports should be designed using TELON conventions (e.g. a Screen Name should be 6 characters, screen fields should not start in column 1, etc.).

The Interface translates Screen and Report Designs into TELON's format and exports them in a transfer file, which in turn can be imported directly into TELON's Design Facility.

Once the basic Screen Designs are in TELON, you may refine the details using TELON's Design Facility. Then TELON's Application Generator and Testing facilities can be used to generate executable code. You should then test the actual screen behavior (editing, computation, database retrieval) and test the screen-to-screen flow, with representative users.

EXCELERATOR

XL/Interface for Micro Focus Workbench

This is an optional interface ($650) which enables you to extract information from an EXCELERATOR specification and transfer it to the Micro Focus COBOL Workbench, where (still on the PC/AT or PS/2) you can use it as the basis for writing, testing, and debugging mainframe COBOL programs.

The Micro Focus Interface does two major things:

1. **Converts structure charts to skeleton COBOL code,** in which a higher-level function will PERFORM a COBOL SECTION for each lower-level function on the structure chart.

    Anything in the Description field of a Function is put into the relevant SECTION as comments.   So this structure chart

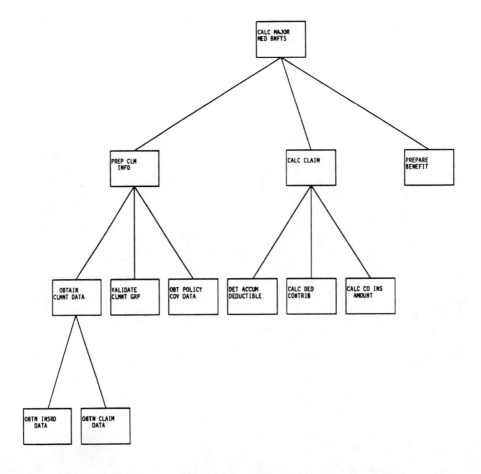

might be converted into a skeleton program starting like this:

```
********************************************************************
*
* SKELETON PROCEDURE DIVISION CREATED FROM AN EXCELERATOR
* STRUCTURE CHART AND PRODUCED BY THE MICRO FOCUS EXCELERATOR
* INTERFACE V1.0.14
*
********************************************************************
      IDENTIFICATION DIVISION.
      PROGRAM-ID. MSTR-MED.
      AUTHOR. XLINT.
      ENVIRONMENT DIVISION.
      CONFIGURATION SECTION.
      SOURCE-COMPUTER. IBM-PC.
      OBJECT-COMPUTER. IBM-PC.
      DATA DIVISION.
      FILE SECTION.
      WORKING-STORAGE SECTION.
      LINKAGE SECTION.
      PROCEDURE DIVISION.

      CALC-MAJOR-MED-BNFTS SECTION.

* Top level control section for major medical program's principal
* calculation process
           PERFORM  PREP-CLM-INFO.
           PERFORM  CALC-CLAIM.
           PERFORM  PREPARE-BENEFIT.
           STOP RUN.

      PREP-CLM-INFO SECTION.

* These sections is responsible for gathering all the appropriate
* CLAIMANT, POLICY and CLAIM data relevant to the processing that
           PERFORM  OBTAIN-CLMNT-DATA.
           PERFORM  VALIDATE-CLMNT-GRP.
           PERFORM  OBT-POLICY-COV-DATA.
           EXIT.

      CALC-CLAIM SECTION.

* This section calculates the amount of the claim included by poli
* coverage.
           PERFORM  DET-ACCUM-DEDUCTIBLE.
           PERFORM  CALC-DED-CONTRIB.
           PERFORM  CALC-CO-INS-AMOUNT.
           EXIT.

      PREPARE-BENEFIT SECTION.

* This section calculates the amount payable to insured based on t
* calculations and resulting disposition records.
           EXIT.

      OBTAIN-CLMNT-DATA SECTION.
* This section collects information regarding insured, claimant an
           PERFORM  OBTN-INSRD-DATA.
           PERFORM  OBTN-CLAIM-DATA.
           EXIT.

      VALIDATE-CLMNT-GRP SECTION.

* This section validates the claimant policy.  The group, policy,
* effective dates are verified.
```

EXCELERATOR

2. **Generates DATA DIVISION entries from Screen Designs, Report Designs, and Records.**

The Micro Focus Interface extracts information from XLDICTIONARY and uses it to build COBOL data definitions. For example, this Screen Design

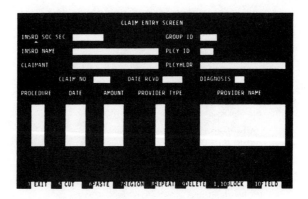

might generate this COBOL 01:

```
*Record CLAIMIN Compiled: 18-DEC-87
01  CLAIMIN.
    05  SSNO        PIC 9(9).
    05  GRPNO       PIC 99999.
    05  LSTNAME     PIC X(25).
    05  PLCYNO      PIC 9999.
    05  CLMNAME     PIC X(25).
    05  PLCYNAM     PIC X(25).
    05  CLMNO       PIC 99999.
    05  RCVDATE     PIC 9(6).
    05  DIAGID      PIC X(3).
    05  PROCEED     OCCURS 6 TIMES.
        10  PROCNO      PIC 9(4).
        10  PROCDATE    PIC 9(6).
        10  PROCCHG     PIC ZZ9.99.
        10  PROVTYPE    PIC X.
        10  PROVNAME    PIC X(25).
```

Document Generation

EXCELERATOR helps you produce specification documents for review.

A document can contain any combination of:

- an extract from the Repository (XLDICTIONARY)

- a diagram

- a Screen or Report Design layout (image)

- any report produced by EXCELERATOR, e.g. Repository analysis

- ASCII files from external word processing or project management packages.

If you select DOCUMENTATION from the main menu, these 4 options are displayed:

Document Graph
allows you to build up a diagram which shows the structure of the document; a visible table of contents, which will be used to generate the documentation (see next page).

Document Production
verifies that all the components specified in the Document Graph are available to you, and prints the document (or writes it to a file).

Word Processing
lets you access Microsoft WORD (or certain other word processing packages) without leaving EXCELERATOR, so that you can create text files (e.g. dealing with business background, system objectives, and so on), and include them in EXCELERATOR documents.

Project Management
lets you access Microsoft PROJECT (or certain other project management packages) without leaving EXCELERATOR, for project planning, scheduling, and tracking. Outputs from the project management package (e.g. status reports) can be included in EXCELERATOR documents.

A Document Graph shows the structure of a document as a tree structure with the root at the left of the diagram, as shown on the next page:

EXCELERATOR

Sample Document Graph:

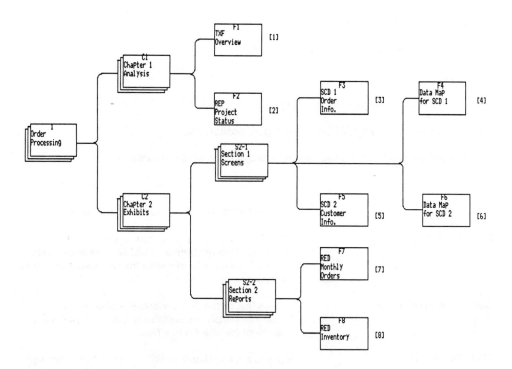

The multi-sheet objects (such as 1:Order Processing) are called Document Groups, and represent parts of documents (in the case of the root, the whole document).

The single-sheet objects (such as F1:TXF Overview) are called Document Fragments, and represent actual pieces of printed output. A Fragment can itself be a lower-level Document Graph, the contents of which make up the fragment.

Desktop publishing interfaces

EXCELERATOR documents can be exported to the Ventura desktop publishing package, and to Postscript printers (such as the Apple Laserwriter).

Project management

Other than the interface to Microsoft PROJECT, EXCELERATOR has no explicit facilities for estimating, planning, scheduling, tracking progress, or version control.

Within the Housekeeping facility, a Project Manager option allows a person with suitable sign-on privileges to

- create a new project, and specify where the Repository will be held.

- assign EXCELERATOR users to projects and set up their access privileges (Read, Limited, or Master).

- look at or delete an existing project, or list all the projects.

- specify whether DFDs should use the Gane/Sarson or Yourdon/DeMarco notation.

- specify default font sizes and object sizes for hardcopy printout.

Design Assistance

Other than the reports which can be generated analyzing the contents of the Repository, EXCELERATOR offers no explicit assistance with design.

EXCELERATOR

Housekeeping

EXCELERATOR has a Housekeeping facility, which provides for

- adding, modifying, or deleting a project.

- backing up a project to archival storage, and restoring it to hard disk.

- adding a user.

- changing a user's privileges or password.

- assigning a user to a new project.

- deleting a user.

- adding a printer or plotter to the system.

- changing printer defaults.

- changing the system date or time.

Suggested standards

XL/Quickstart (first-copy price $2000) provides suggestions for standards to follow on a project, such as conventions for labelling and numbering Processes, for defining Data Relationships, for maintaining a set of standard abbreviations, and so on.

EXCELERATOR

Hardware/software platforms

MS-DOS machines:

AT&T 6300
Compaq Plus, Portable 286, Portable III
HP Vectra
IBM PC/AT, PC/XT, 3270 PC Model 6, 3270 AT Model 79, PS/2 Models 50 and 60

On most machines, EXCELERATOR needs 640K (software actually takes 490K) and 10Mb disk.

LANs supported include	3COM Ethernet IBM PC Network Banyan Vines
Printers supported include	Epson FX100, LQ1500 HP Laserjet + IBM 80 CPS Graphics, Proprinter QMS 800, 1200 TI 855 Toshiba 1350, 1351, P351
Plotters supported include	HP 7475A, 7470A

Copy protection is through a hardware block in the parallel port.

VAX/VMS machines:

DEC   VAXstation II, Micro VAX II, VAX
VMS   4.4 and above, Decnet network

Other workstations:

SUN-3

Apollo   DN3000

EXCELERATOR

Vendor support

Education:

Class	Duration	Prerequisites
EXCELERATOR Fundamentals	2 days	Familiarity with structured techniques
Implementing EXCELERATOR	3 days	Proficiency in EXCELERATOR

(Other classes are available for EXCELERATOR/RTS.)

Newsletter: Quarterly newsletter, "InTechniques"

Toll-free hotline: Quality of response is generally praised by users

Consulting support: Referral to firms who are in the Associated Consultants program

User Group donated software:

XL/Group, the User Group, provides some software free of charge on an as-is, non-supported basis. Programs available include:

IMS DB/DC Link	Two-way exchange of data between EXCELERATOR XL/DICTIONARY and IBM mainframe
IDMS/IDD Interface	Two-way exchange of data between EXCELERATOR XL/DICTIONARY and Cullinet's data dictionary
DATAMANAGER Interface	Two-way exchange of data between EXCELERATOR XL/DICTIONARY and MSP's mainframe data dictionary
DB2 Download	Downloads table definitions from DB2 Catalog into Records and Elements in XL/DICTIONARY

PART III

Product Summaries

This part consists of summaries of 24 representative product lines, covering 82 products in all, arranged so that all the facts about each product line are presented in a standard comparable way in a single double-page spread.

Each Product Summary covers

- vendor's address and phone number(s).
- the hardware/software platform(s) that support the product.
- the minimum PC configuration, where relevant.
- the first-copy price. (It is industry practice to offer steep discounts for multiple-copy orders, and for site or corporate licenses.)

For each product, the report has an entry dealing with

- the diagram types that the product supports.
- whether or not the diagram symbols and syntax rules can be modified by the users.
- any significant limitations on the diagrams.
- the objects that can be stored in the Repository (design database).
- how the Repository is integrated with the graphics facility (where relevant), and how it is integrated with mainframe Repositories (supplied by the vendor or from other sources).
- what provision the product makes for allowing more than one user to share the Repository at a given time. Some products allow only one user at a time, some provide for locking of a part of the Repository, and some allow a user to update one object while another user is updating another object on the same diagram.
- the facility for producing reports which list contents of the Repository in various ways.
- the facility for prototyping screens and reports.
- the facility for code generation.
- the facility for generating documents in various formats.
- any facility for supporting a project manager.
- any built-in assistance with design, such as an interactive dialog for normalization.
- the vendor's statement of direction.
- figures supplied by the vendor, or gleaned from industry sources, on 1987 and 1988 revenues, the vendor's installed base at the end of 1988, and 1989 projections.

Product Summary   Analyst/Designer Toolkit

A/DT is a relatively low-cost product supporting Yourdon/DeMarco requirements definition and structured design.

Runs on:	*AT, PS/2*	**Vendor:**	*Yourdon Inc.*
			1501 Broadway, Suite 601
Min. config.:	*640K, 10Mb, mouse,*		*New York, NY 10036*
	Hercules monochrome		*212/391-2828*
Price:	*$2495 for first copy*		

GRAPHICS:

Diagram types: *DFD, ERD, State-transition diag, Structure charts, Context diags, Presentation diags.*

User-modify: -

Limitations: -

REPOSITORY: (Uses dBASE III)

Objects: *Data element, data structure, process, data flow, terminator, data stores, entity, relationship, state, module, requirement.*

How integrated: *with graphics:*   *Interactive access between diagrams and dictionary.*

            with mainframe: *Convert dictionary to ASCII with dBASE III, and do file transfer, and/or convert diagrams directly to ASCII with Extract function.*

Control of sharing: *At discretion of users; no explicit locking.*

Analysis reports: *Standard reports available; users can write custom reports with dBASE III.*

PROTOTYPING: *No screen-painter.*

CODE GENERATION: *No.*

/ continued

DOCUMENT GENERATION:

COMPOSE facility is included in toolkit.
Optional HP Laserjet support ($150).

PROJECT MGMT SUPPORT: *None explicit.*

DESIGN ASSISTANCE: *None.*

OTHER FEATURES:

Uses CADWARE Design Graphics system for creation of graphics.
Back-annotation feature allows ASCII Extract file to be edited for modification of text on diagram.

VENDOR DIRECTION:

LAN support.
Expand dictionary for user-defined objects.   Postscript driver.
Windowing: User-definable data entry screens.
Generations of preliminary data models from DFD.

MARKET SHARE:

1987 sales:	*1000 units (implying revenues of approx. $2 million).*
1988 sales:	*2000 units (implying revenues of approx. $4 million).*
Installed base at end of 1988:	*Approx. 3000 units.*
1989 projected sales:	*Not available, but thought to be in 2000 unit range.*

USER GROUP: *Not yet.*

A low-cost tool for creating DFDs, data dictionary, and process specification on the Macintosh.

Runs on:	*Macintosh*	**Vendor:**	*Advanced Logical Software*
			9903 Santa Monica Blvd., Suite 108
Min. config:	*512K, external drive*		*Beverly Hills, CA 90212*
Price:	*$925 for first copy*		*213/653-5786*

GRAPHICS:

Diagram types: *DFDs.*

User-modify: *No.*

Limitations: *Not more than 15 processes per diagram, not more than 200 symbols overall. 9 levels of explosion supported.*

REPOSITORY:

Objects: *Basic data, alias, data structure, data store, known data.*

How integrated: *with graphics:*   *Automatic.*
                              with mainframe: *Export data dictionary as ASCII file.*
                                                      MIX utility allows merging of data dictionaries.

Control of sharing: *N/A.*

Analysis reports: *List repository contents by type. Print out Repository contents showing hierarchy. Consistency checking reports.*

PROTOTYPING: *None.*

CODE GENERATION: *None.*

DOCUMENT GENERATION: *DFD(s) and details can be printed out in standard document format.*

/ continued

ANATOOL

PROJECT MGMT SUPPORT: *None explicit.*

DESIGN ASSISTANCE: *None.*

OTHER FEATURES: *Specifications can be exported to MacDesigner (from Excel Software).*

VENDOR DIRECTION: *Multi-user capability.*
User customization.
Real-time SA support, Prototyping, Design support, Code generation.
(Vendor is US subsidiary of French company.)

MARKET SHARE:

1987 sales:	*300 units (implying revenues of approx. $250,000).*
1988 sales:	*600 units (implying revenues of approx. $600,000).*
Installed base at end of 1988:	*1000 copies.*
1989 projected sales:	*1500 copies (implying revenues of approx. $1,500,000).*

USER GROUP: *Not yet.*

Product Summary — APS Development Center

The APS Development Center provides a powerful, integrated family of application generators, starting from the point where requirements, data, and program specifications have been defined. It has no diagramming or data analysis capability (though it does have a direct interface with EXCELERATOR); the programmer defines data, screens, reports, and program flow, and APS generates COBOL for a wide range of environments. Definition, programming, and code generation can be done entirely on the PC (or on a VM/MVS terminal).

Runs on:	APS/PC Workstation: PS/2-70+	Vendor:	Sage Software
	Mainframe Painters, dictionary and		3200 Monroe Street
	generators: MVS/TSO/ISPF.		Rockville, MD 20852
	Can also have Painters and		301/230-3200
	Sub-dictionary under VM/CMS.		800/638-8703

Min. PC config.: APS/PC: 640K, 3Mb extended memory, 5Mb disk, Microfocus COBOL/2

Prices:		
First copy of APS/PC	$5000 - $8000, depending on features
PC-MVS link	$10,000
MVS painters	$25,000
On-Line Express	$20,000
Code generators	$15,000 - $35,000, depending on options
Importers	$5000 - $15,000, depending on options
DB2 Data Base Painter	$15,000
On-Screen Documentation	$10,000
Customization Facility:	$75,000

GRAPHICS: None, but can accept entity-lists from EXCELERATOR into PC Sub-dictionary with EXCELERATOR Integrator ($6000 site license).

PAINTERS:

Application Painter:	Focal point for associating application entities, generating/documenting systems.
Screen Painter:	Non-procedural definition/maintenance of screen formats, attribute and edit criteria, generation parameters.
Report Mock-Up Painter:	Non-procedural definition/maintenance of report formats at layout level.
Scenario Prototype Painter:	Build up and exercise screen-to-screen flow; modify interactively.
Data Structure Painter:	Non-procedural definition of data structures.
On-line Express Painter:	Non-procedural, fill-in-the-blanks application generator for standard on-line procedure development and maintenance.
Program Painter:	Semi-procedural support for program development and maintenance.

/continued

APS Development Center

REPOSITORY: (called APS Application Dictionary)

Objects: *PC Workstation:*   *Holds objects created with Painters, and imported from front-end tools, PC-targeted and generated code.*

     Mainframe: *Holds objects created with Painters plus generated/imported program module/database objects.*

How integrated: *with graphics:*   *Not applicable.*

     with mainframe: *PC/MVS link provides dictionary-to-dictionary communications.*

Control of sharing: *PC/MVS link provides for check-out/-in of entities, with date-time stamp.*

Analysis reports: *Wide range of cross-reference, dictionary listings, etc.*

PROTOTYPING:
(PC or mainframe)   *Screen Painter can build/exercise screens. Scenario Prototype Painter can exercise screen-to-screen flow. ISPF prototyping (mainframe) can exercise logic flow and data access. Additional: PC targeted code can be prototyped with Microfocus products.*

CODE GENERATION:

Generates COBOL or COBOL II for batch, IMS DB/DC, CICS environments, accessing DB2, DL/1, VSAM, and IDMS. Can generate DB2 object definitions. Optional DB2 Data Base Painter non-procedurally defines DB2 objects, allowing impact analysis, comprehensive documentation, and object generation capabilities.

DOCUMENT GENERATION: *As a by-product of code generation.*

PROJECT MGMT SUPPORT: *None explicit.*

DESIGN ASSISTANCE: *Physical design support through non-procedural painters.*

OTHER FEATURES: *Can reverse engineer IMS DBDs, VSAM file definitions, DB2 catalogs and BMS screen maps into APS Application Dictionary. On-screen Documentation Facility makes APS manuals available on-line, with searches by topic, keyword, etc.*

VENDOR DIRECTION: *Distributed Development: Strategic Alliances e.g. w/Perot Systems. Broader functional coverage across the development life cycle.*

MARKET SHARE: *1987 sales:*   *53 units (implying revenues of approx. $10 million).*

     1988 sales: *70-80 units (implying revenues of approx. $15 million).*

     Installed base at end of 1988: Approx. 200 installations.

     1989 projections: Approx. $17 million.

USER GROUP: *The APS User Group. For info contact Patty Voyles*
     Lockheed Aircraft
     Burbank, CA
     Phone: 818/847-7323

BACHMAN
Product Set

Charles Bachman and his team are building a very powerful integrated set of expert-system-products starting from the idea that reverse engineering of existing code and data definitions into a logical model is as important as forward engineering from requirements to code. Five of the products (Data Analyst, DB2 Database Administrator, IDMS Database Administrator, IMS Capture, and Files Capture) are available at the date of this report; the others are scheduled for release over the next two years. The full product set will include:

Data Analyst: BACHMAN/DA	Supports information modelling and logical database design using Bachman Entity Relationship diagrams. Builds Repository, or starts from a design re-engineered from DBA products. The design advisor ensures a normalized design.
Database Administrators: BACHMAN/DBA (IDMS) BACHMAN/DBA (DB2) BACHMAN/Capture (IMS) BACHMAN/Capture (Files)	Each DBA is an expert system which can capture data description language source and present it in a graphical editor. From that point, it may be edited or re-engineered to the specification level for use in the DA products. A specification level design from the DA product may be forward engineered into one of the DBA products. Using the DBA product, the design may be validated and run against the expert designer, and can be generated back into DDL source ready for the mainframe.
Systems Analyst: BACHMAN/SA	Support for DFDs, other high-level system modelling diagrams. Reverse engineering of actual systems to their appropriate components.
Programmer Assistant: BACHMAN/PA	Expert system for Reverse engineering of COBOL to specification, working as "co-pilot" with programmer. Generates COBOL from specification language and Repository.

Runs on:	Compaq 386, PS/2 Model 80	**Vendor:**	Bachman Information Systems
Min. config.:	10 Mb RAM, 20 Mb disk,		Four Cambridge Center
	Moniterm Viking or IBM 8514		Cambridge, MA 02142
Price:	$25,000 for first copy of package,		617/354-1414
	including Data Analyst and a DBA.		
	Additional DBA $10,000.		

GRAPHICS: (In DA and DBA: other products graphics not yet defined.)
Diagram types: BACHMAN Entity Relationship Diagram
BACHMAN Diagram (IDMS Schema Diagram)
BACHMAN DB2 Relational and DB2 Physical Diagrams.
User-modify: No.
Limitations: -

/continued

BACHMAN
Product Set

REPOSITORY:

Objects: *DA: entities, attributes, relationships, keys, dimensions, domains, data-types.*
DBA (IDMS): records, sets, areas, schemas, items, files, procedures.
DBA (DB2): tables, table spaces, columns, indexes.

How integrated: *with graphics:*   *Immediate update. Diagram is drawn from Repository entries with manual or automatic placement and automatic routing algorithm for objects and connectors.*
                 with mainframe: *File transfer.*

Control of sharing: *Not yet determined.*

Analysis reports: *Real-time messages from expert advisory system on completeness and consistency of model.*

PROTOTYPING: *No separate prototyping facility; generate code and exercise actual system.*

CODE GENERATION: *DB2 and IDMS DBAs generate complete optimized DDL for target DBMS.*

DOCUMENT GENERATION: *Data models and Repository entries can be printed and plotted.*
Design reasoning is logged for later review.

PROJECT MGMT SUPPORT: *None explicit.*

DESIGN ASSISTANCE: *Extensive: Each product contains expert advisory system to act as "design assistant," e.g. in database design. Analyst can choose to have very detailed explanations and suggestions displayed as the expert system operates, or to have explanations suppressed.*

OTHER FEATURES: *Hypertext style forms entry system for defining and modifying details of repository.*

VENDOR DIRECTION: *Complete development of product line.*

MARKET SHARE:

1987 sales: *Not on market.*
1988 sales (5 months):   *100 units (implying revenues of approx. $2.5 million).*
Installed base at end of 1988:   *100 units.*
1989 projected sales: *Not available; (thought to be approx. 300 units, with revenues in $10 million range).*

DEC VAX software developers use CorVision's integrated-CASE tools to automate the major phases of the software lifecycle (design, specification, generation, and maintenance) for VAX MIS applications which employ RMS and Rdb data management systems. The design tools, including entity, dataview, menu and action diagrammers, and screen and report painters are resident on a PC workstation (AT or PS/2 compatible) close-coupled with a specification central repository and generator on a VAX. The generator produces complete applications compiled to a native VMS executable image, which can be run on any VAX/VMS machine, together with full system documentation.

Runs on:	Workstation: PC, PS/2, AT, VT terminals	**Vendor:**	Cortex Corp.
	Repository & Generator: VAX		138 Technology Dr.
Min. config.:	640K, 20 Mb, mouse, CGA		Waltham, MA 02154
Price:	$55K-250K for development license		617/894-7000

GRAPHICS:
Called "Picture Programming" tools
Diagram types: ERD, Menu diag., Dataview diag., action diag.
User-modify: No.
Limitations: -

REPOSITORY:
Objects: PC: Nothing is stored on the workstation.

VAX: Diagrams, source code, object code, system documentation.

How integrated: with graphics: Real time update; PC workstation is continuously on-line to VAX.

Control of sharing: Locked for update at object level.

Analysis reports: Completeness and consistency is checked in real time.

PROTOTYPING:
No separate capability, since dialogs can be exercised using generated code.

CODE GENERATION:
Generates optimized native VMS executable machine-code for multi-user VAX applications using RMS or Rdb.

95%-98% of all application requirements can typically be met through Cor Vision.

/continued

Cor Vision

Custom code for specialized logic, e.g. specialized calculations or interfaces, can be written in CorVision's VHLL BUILDER or in any DEC supported language.

The procedural logic can be structured using the action diagrammer.

DOCUMENT GENERATION: *System documentation generated by application generator; diagrams can also be printed.*

PROJECT MGMT SUPPORT: *Dynamic status screen lists parts of application that are completed or need to be completed.*

DESIGN ASSISTANCE: *Intelligent Guidance system; recommends next logical step in development.*

Cor Vision knows what remains unfinished from user's last session and can provide "what if" and impact analysis information.

OTHER FEATURES: *Generated applications can run on any VAX and can interface to DEC's VIA layered products.*

VENDOR DIRECTION: *High-level analysis tools.*
Support other relational DBMs.
End-user documentation.

MARKET SHARE:

1987 sales AF (12 months):	*Revenue $7 million.*
1988 sales:	*Revenue thought to be in the $12 million range.*
Installed base at end of 1988:	*Approx. 1000 run-time applications, 250 development copies at 150 sites.*
1989 projected sales:	*Thought to be in the $15 million range.*

USER GROUP: *CORUS. For information, contact Howard Exton-Smith at Cortex.*

Product Summary   **Deft**

Deft Inc. specializes in the provision of CASE tools to users of relational database management systems (rdbms). Deft uses a Macintosh to build a model, which is then uploaded to various rdbms on a variety of hardware platforms.

Runs on: *Macintosh workstation.*   **Vendor:**   *DEFT INC.*
                      Central repository and target on   *557 Dixon Rd, Suite 110*
                      VAX/VMS, ULTRIX, IBM AS400,   *Rexdale, ON M9W 1H7*
                      TANDEM, IBM/MVS/ADABAS, UNIX   *CANADA*
                                                                       416/249-2246

Min. workstation
 config.:   *MacPlus*
Price: *Macintosh: $9,000 for first copy*
                      VAX: $10,000 - $52,000 depending on size

GRAPHICS:

Diagram types: *DFD (Gane/Sarson, Yourdon/DeMarco notations), E-RD, Jackson Structure diagram, Form and Report Layouts*
User-modify: *No.*
Limitations: *-*

REPOSITORY: *(called Deft Central Dictionary; uses rdbms)*
Objects: *All diagram objects.*

How integrated: *with graphics:*   *Automatic as object entered on diagram.*
                      with mainframe: *Upload to ORACLE, Rdb, INGRES, SYBASE, ADABAS and NON-STOP-SQL.*
                                           Can reverse engineer from INGRES.

Control of sharing: *Multi-user update and retrieval capability via a file-server-based rdbms repository.*

Analysis reports: *Each editor produces analysis report. Reports may be fed directly to PageMaker. User may tailor the PageMaker style tags so that reports will assume any desired formats.*

PROTOTYPING: *Formatter module allows screen/report design. Screen can be exercised through application generation on VAX.*

CODE GENERATION: *Translator module on VAX (VMS and ULTRIX) can generate INGRES database definitions, and INGRES VIFRED (Visual Forms Editor) screen generation definitions.*
                         Generator module on VAX can interface direct to Software AG's CONSTRUCT Application Generator.
                         Link to FOUNDATION DBMS on Tandem.

/ continued

DOCUMENT GENERATION: *Diagram and definitions can be exported to PageMaker, MS-WORD, MacDraw, and other desktop publishing packages.*

PROJECT MANAGEMENT SUPPORT: *None explicit.*

DESIGN ASSISTANCE: *None explicit.*

OTHER FEATURES: *Deft Configuration Management System establishes software libraries under VAX/VMS for code modules and object libraries.*

Seamless interface from Macintosh to VAX-based applications.

VENDOR DIRECTION: *Support for DB2 and broader UNIX base. Code generation of workstation-based applications.*

MARKET SHARE:

1987 sales:	*50 copies (implying revenues of approx $500,000).*
1988 sales:	*125 copies (implying revenues of approx. $1.25 million).*
Installed base at end of 1988:	*Approx. 425 copies at approx. 85 sites.*
1989 projected sales:	*250 copies (implying revenues of approx. $2.5 million).*

USER GROUP: *For information, contact Eric Goldman at DEFT.*

Product Summary   DESIGN / 1

DESIGN/1 is the PC-based design support product of the FOUNDATION product line, which also includes METHOD/1, a PC-based automated project management support tool, and INSTALL/1, a mainframe-based central Repository.

Runs on:	*XT, AT*	**Vendor:**	*Arthur Andersen & Co.*
			33 West Monroe
Min. config.:	*512K, 2 floppies*		*Chicago, IL 60602*
	more optional, EGA?		*312/580-0033*
Price:	*$7000 for first copy*		

GRAPHICS:

Diagram types: *DFD (Yourdon/DeMarco notations), ERD (Chen notation), Warnier-Orr diags, flowcharts.*

User-modify: *No.*

Limitations: *450 characters wide by 450 lines high.*

REPOSITORY:

Objects: *PC workstation:*   *All diagram objects, data elements/structures, entities/relationships, diagram cross-references, screen/report descriptions, conversation prototypes, generalized documents.*

      Mainframe: (INSTALL/1):   *Data dictionary, test data.*

How integrated: *with graphics:*   *Updated when diagram is saved.*

      with mainframe: *Upload from DESIGN/1 to INSTALL/1 or IBM DB/DC dictionary or Cullinet IDD.*

Control of sharing: *Documents locked for update.*

Analysis reports: *Extensive reporting on Repository contents.*

PROTOTYPING: *Screen and Report Design Aid helps develop layouts.*
Conversation Prototyping facility enables data to be entered into screens and screen-to-screen flow to be exercised.

CODE GENERATION: *Generate COBOL 01s and BMS maps.*
Generate DB2 database definitions.
Generate IDMS database definitions.

/ continued

DESIGN / 1

DOCUMENT GENERATION: *All design documents can be printed.*

PROJECT MANAGEMENT SUPPORT: *METHOD/1 ($50,000 for site licence) (requires 20Mb disk) provides for customized project task list, automated estimating support, time reporting, status report generation, and change reporting.*

DESIGN ASSISTANCE: *None explicit in DESIGN/1.*
INSTALL/1 ($200,000 for CPU licence) provides DB2 performance analysis.

OTHER FEATURES: *User interface very easy to learn.*

VENDOR DIRECTION: *Further integration between DESIGN/1, INSTALL/1, and METHOD/1.*

MARKET SHARE: *Not available.*

USER GROUP: *No.*

Product Summary   # THE DEVELOPER

A PC-based analyst/designer/project manager workbench (front-end CASE tool). Supports strategic I.S. planning, data and process modelling, requirements definition, analysis, design, prototyping, program specification and project management activities for business and real-time systems development. THE DEVELOPER uses SQL to access its PC-based repository or THE INTEGRATER (Central Repository Facility) running on the mainframe under DB/2 or ORACLE. The workbench characteristics (graphic objects, diagram types, documentation screens layouts, etc.) are customizable.

Runs on:	*(PC workstation) XT/AT*	**Vendor:**	*ASYST Technologies Inc.*
	3270 PC, 286, 386		*One Naperville Plaza*
	(Mainframe) MVS/TSO with DB2 or ORACLE		*Naperville, IL 60540*
	VAX/VMS with ORACLE		*312/416-2990*
Min. config.:	*640K, 10 Mb, mouse*		
Price:	*$5400 for first copy*		
	Mainframe repository $30,000-$50,000		

GRAPHICS:

Diagram types: *DFD (Yourdon/DeMarco and Gane/Sarson notations), ERD (Chen, Bachman and Merise notations), Structure chart, Organization chart (decomposition diags.), Operation Procedures diags., ten different types of matrix diags., System flowchart, all provided as standard.*

User-modify: *See Objects below.*

Limitations: *Diagrams are made with text symbols (graphitext); size is limited to 222 characters wide x 66 characters high (approx. 9 screens). (To be upgraded.)*

REPOSITORY:

(called THE INTEGRATER (Central Repository Facility) on the mainframe) SQL based relational DBMS (currently MDBS in relational mode on PC, DB/2 and ORACLE on mainframe). PC and mainframe Repository accessible in real-time.

Objects: *50 (called Components: Data element, data flow, data store, process, etc.) and 22 relationship types (is input to, is used by, etc.) provided as standard. With THE CUSTOMIZER, users can define their own or modify existing objects or relationship types, relationship rules, and the screens to document these objects. PC and mainframe encyclopedia can equally be customized.*

How integrated: *with graphics:*   *Synchronization process analyzes a diagram, compares it with Repository, updates Repository as necessary.*

                    with mainframe: *One task interacts with PC Repository and the other task with the mainframe Repository in real-time. Any information on either Repository can be copied on the other in real-time.*

Control of sharing: *Application, release, and object-level locking of Repository.*

Analysis reports: *Menu-driven SQL queries of workstation/mainframe repository. Syntax validation.*

/ continued

THE DEVELOPER

PROTOTYPING: *Screen/report painter integrated with Repository.*
Screens cannot be exercised.

CODE GENERATION: *Export of the application, database, and text specifications*
contained in the repository to be used as input to a code
generator. Links to SAGE-APS, Zanthe-ZIM.

DOCUMENT GENERATION: *Deliverable (report, specifications, etc.) Generator*
enables user to list document content (text, diagram,
forms, reports, screens, etc.) in table of contents.
Document is assembled automatically. Export to Ventura.

PROJECT MGMT SUPPORT: *Project tracking query, customizable Repository objects*
to support project management documentation and
reporting using Deliverable Generator.

DESIGN ASSISTANCE: *None imbedded in the tool. ASYST Technologies offers*
MINI-ASYST as companion application development and
project managment life-cycle methodology.

OTHER FEATURES: *On-line tutorial included. Import/Export. Same text editor*
used in graphic and text mode.

VENDOR DIRECTION: *Provide highly-customizable integrated environment from*
strategic I.S. planning through to code generation. Repository
support for human generated specifications. Reverse
engineering input to repository.

MARKET SHARE:

1987 sales: *200 units (implying revenues of approx. $1 million).*
1988 sales: *700 units (implying revenues of approx. $3.5 million).*
Installed base at end of 1988:   *1000 copies at more than 100 sites.*
1989 projected sales: *1500 workstations, 15 central repositories (implying revenues of*
approx. $8 million).

THE DEVELOPER, THE INTEGRATER, THE CUSTOMIZER, and MINI-ASYST are trademarks of
ASYST Technologies Inc.

Product Summary   ER-DESIGNER (ERD)

ERD is a low-cost data modelling tool which feeds into Chen's other products: Normalizer, which helps in data analysis, SchemaGen, which produces database definitions, and DDS-Link, which uploads the PC Repository to mainframe dictionaries.

Runs on:	*XT/AT*	**Vendor:** *Chen & Associates*
Min. config.:	*320K, 2 floppies,*	*4884 Constitution Ave, Ste 1E*
Price:	*$495 for first copy of ERD*	*Baton Rouge, LA 70808*
		504/928-5765

GRAPHICS:
Diagram types: *ERD (Chen or Martin notation).*

User-modify: *No.*
Limitations: *Number of entities and attributes limited by memory, e.g. 640K - 300 defined objects with average 10 attributes. Max. 128 attributes per object.*

REPOSITORY:
Objects: *Entities, Entity Attributes, Relationship, Relationship Attribute, Connection, Cardinality, Comment.*

How integrated: *With graphics:*   *automatic -- user is prompted to fill in details of each object. Repository updated thru diag.*

         With mainframe: *DDS-Link product ($995) uploads to IBM DB/DC Dictionary, DATAMANAGER, DESIGNMANAGER, IDD/IDMS, DATACOM via file-transfer.*

Control of sharing: *At model level or entity level.*

Analysis reports: *Print ERD and list Repository contents.*
                        ReportGen allows selection of entries.

PROTOTYPING: *No.*

CODE GENERATION:
     SchemaGen ($495 for dBASE, $995 for INGRES, ORACLE, $1995 for DB2, SQL/DS, IDMS, IDS, DATACOM, MODEL 204, DMS2, DMS1100, $3995 for IMS) will generate database definition statements.

/continued

ER-DESIGNER (ERD)

DOCUMENT GENERATION: *Report Gen feature.*

PROJECT MGMT SUPPORT: *None explicit.*

DESIGN ASSISTANCE:

Normalizer product ($1495) reads Repository.   User selects data structure and enters functional dependencies;   Normalizer breaks down structure into 3NF relations.

OTHER FEATURES: *Interfaces to Design Aid ($295 for first copy).*
Interfaces to EXCELERATOR ($295 for first copy).
Interfaces to IEW ($295 for first copy).

VENDOR DIRECTION: *Name analysis; implement naming conventions.*
Expert system for E-R modelling.
Reverse engineering of IMS, IDMS, and IDS to ERD.
Generate database definitions for other DBMSs.

MARKET SHARE:

1987 sales:	*300 units (implying revenues of approx. $500,000).*
1988 sales:	*Approx. 300 units (implying revenues of approx. $500,000).*
Installed base at end of 1988:	*600 copies.*
1989 projected sales:	*Approx. 600 units (implying revenues of approx. $1 million).*

USER GROUP: *Not yet.*

Product Summary   EXCELERATOR

EXCELERATOR is a PC-based product with extensive graphical modelling capability. It uses semantic color, integrated with a repository stored on the PC disk. Graphical symbols and syntax can be user-modified with an extra-charge upgrade. Screen and report layouts can be prototyped and execution simulated to a limited extent. Screen layouts and data definitions can be exported to several code-generators marketed by other firms (e.g. Pansophic's TELON). It also provides extensive project management support.

Runs on:	*XT/AT/VAX/SUN/Apollo*	**Vendor:**	*Index Technology*
			1 Main Street
Min. config.:	*640K, 10Mb, mouse, EGA*		*Cambridge, MA 02142*
Price:	*$8400 for first copy*		*617/494-8200*

Also markets EXCELERATOR/RTS for modelling real time systems and PC/PRISM for planning.

GRAPHICS:

Diagram types: *DFD, ERD/Data model diag, Structure chart/structure diagram, Document graph, Presentation diag (IBM flowchart), State-transition diagram (RTS), Matrix graph (RTS).*

User-modify: *With added-cost ($12,500) Customizer product (can be rented for $2,000 per month).*

Limitations: -

REPOSITORY:

Objects: *45 (Data store, record, element, process, etc.). See Part II.*

How integrated: *Diagram objects must be explicitly entered into Repository. Changes to Repository appear on diagrams. Repository feeds/can be updated from screen-painter. Changes to Repository don't automatically appear on existing screens. Can export Repository as ASCII file.*

Control of sharing: *Parts or all of main repository can be exported as sub-projects; such parts can be locked and cannot be modified until unlocked (typically by authorized import of revised sub-project information). Multi-level authorization and password control. Interactive sharing of joint repository on VAX.*

Analysis reports: *Many standard reports, with wildcard request facility.*

PROTOTYPING: *Interactively build up screens/report layouts. Can enter data into defined screen - field-level edits operate, can update a file from screen, but cannot query the file.*

/continued

EXCELERATOR

CODE GENERATION: *Data definitions/ screen maps in COBOL, BASIC, C, PL/1 Interface to TELON code generator (XL/Interface TELON, $9000 for site license), MICROFOCUS COBOL Workbench ($650). Sage Software APS code generator has interface to EXCELERATOR. Structure charts/screens/reports can be exported to Team/Errico for code generation.*

DOCUMENT GENERATION: *Diagrams, repository entries, external ASCII word processing files, can be combined into single printout. PostScript supported. Interface to Ventura desktop publisher, and Interleaf.*

PROJECT MANAGEMENT SUPPORT: *Work breakdown structure diagram. Dictionary entities mapped to project, task. Direct integration with ABTs Project Manager Workbench. Interfaces to other PM packages.*

DESIGN ASSISTANCE: *Consistency checking on diagrams. Analysis of similarity between screen and report designs to flag possible duplication.*

OTHER FEATURES: *AFIPS Software Product of the Year 1987. Index Tech was the first front-end CASE vendor to have a public stock offering.*

VENDOR DIRECTION: *Support entire development process.*
Provide rigorous support for variety of methodologies, eg IDEF.
Facilitate use of reusable system definition components.
Enhance graphics interface using emerging industry standards for windowing. Support OS2/PM and X-Windows.
Provide additional interfaces to a variety of other software products.
Expand support for two-way communication of data from and to the Repository so that it can be kept synchronized with the physical system. Enhance the structure of the Repository.
Provide enhanced networking and multi-user access.
Interface to IBM Repository; SAA compatibility.

MARKET SHARE:

1987 sales:	*6500 units, (revenue $22.9 million).*
1988 sales:	*8500 units (implying revenues of approx. $30 million).*
Installed base at end of 1988:	*14,000 copies at 1600 sites.*
1989 projections:	*Not available; thought to be approx. 11,000 units, with revenue in $40 million range.*

USER GROUP: *XL/GROUP. For information, contact Judith Vanderkay at Index.*

Product Summary

Information Engineering Facility (IEF)

IEF is the most fully integrated CASE product currently available for the IBM environment. It has been developed by a major dedicated effort (said to exceed 100 man-years) within Texas Instruments. It provides automated support for Information Engineering and was developed in conjunction with James Martin's group. Once the data model has been detailed and process logic has been specified with action diagrams, COBOL code can be automatically generated.

Runs on:	*PC workstation*	**Vendor:**	*Texas Instruments*
	DB2 mainframe repository		*PO Bx 869305, Drawer 8474*
Min. config.:	*5 AT-level workstations, DB2*		*Plano, TX 75086*
Price:	*PC workstation:*	*$ 13,900*	*214/575-4404*
	Central encyclopedia:	*$ 70,000*	
	Code generator:	*$140,000*	
	DB2 generator:	*$ 55,000*	

GRAPHICS:

Diagram types: *Matrix diagram, ERD, Entity hierarchy diagram, Process hierarchy diagram, Process dependency diagram, Dialog flow diagram, Screen design diagram, Data structure diagram, Process action diagram, Procedure action diagram. REDRAW command uses internal logic to automatically position objects on diagram.*
Pop-up windows display selected Repository contents while viewing a diagram.

User-modify: *No.*

Limitations: *No DFD. (The Process Dependency diagram shows process interdependency at a higher level of abstraction than a DFD.)*

REPOSITORY:

	Workstation:	*All diagram objects.*
	Central:	*All diagram objects.*

How integrated: *with graphics:*   *SAVE CURRENT MODEL stores diagram in local Repository.*
with mainframe: *UPLOAD/DOWNLOAD command.*

Control of sharing: *Many users can have subsets of a model downloaded for update at any given time. Each workstation operates alone on extract from central Repository; results are merged on UPLOAD.*

Analysis reports: *ISPF reports from Central Repository.*   *Entity Definitions.*
                                                 Function Definitions.

/continued

Information
Engineering Facility (IEF)

PROTOTYPING: *Build up Screen design diagram to see layout; generate code to exercise. Execute generated applications in a TSO testing environment.*

CODE GENERATION: *Process action diagram uses special language to specify logic. Generates VS COBOL II code with DB2 calls, operating under either IMS/DC, CICS, or TSO.*
Generates DB2 database definitions.

DOCUMENT GENERATION: *None explicit.*

PROJECT MGMT SUPPORT: *None.*

DESIGN ASSISTANCE: *Automatic transformation of ERD to user - customized database definitions.*

Automatic transformation of analysis-level processes into detailed procedure definitions.

OTHER FEATURES: *Interactive action-diagram-level debugging under TSO.*

VENDOR DIRECTION: *Function points. Target environments of VM, UNIX.*
Generate code on PC.

MARKET SHARE:

1987 sales:	*Approx. 70 sites, some with code generator.*
	(Revenues of approx. $5 million.)
1988 sales:	*50 installations (revenues of approx. $15 million to $20 million).*
Installed base at end of 1988:	*120 sites.*
1989 projected sales:	*50 installations (revenues of approx. $20 million).*

USER GROUP: *IEF Users Group. For information, call Dale Dukes at Texas Instruments.*

Product Summary   Information
Engineering Workbench (IEW)

IEW is a powerful PC-based product with workstation repository which can optionally be consolidated into a mainframe repository (IEW-MF). IEW generates code via Gamma, its COBOL application generator. It has four components: Planning Workstation, Analysis Workstation, Design Workstation and GAMMA. Each workstation can be used independently.

Runs on:	*IEW/WS: AT, PS/2-50+*	**Vendor:**	*KnowledgeWare Inc.*
	Compaq 286/386,		*3340 Peachtree Road NE*
	GAMMA: MVS, TSO/ISPF, CICS.		*Atlanta, GA 30026*
	IEW/MF: MVS/TSO.		*404/231-8575*
Min. config.:	*640K + 4 Mb expanded or extended memory,*		
	20 Mb disk, high density disk drive,		
	mouse, EGA or VGA		
Price:	*Planning WS, Analyst WS, Design WS:*		*$ 8625 for first copy*
	Starter Kit (one of each WS):		*$ 10,000*
	Mainframe Encyclopedia:		*$115,000*
	GAMMA:		*$209,300*

GRAPHICS: *Uses GEM (from Digital Research, Inc.) for windowing and pull-down menus. Up to six windows can be opened concurrently.*

Diagram types:
Planning WS: *Decomposition diag, ERD, Association Matrix diag, Property Matrix diag.*
Analysis WS: *Decomposition diag, DFD, ERD, Action diag.*
Design WS: *Structure chart diag, Action diag/modules, Screen Layout diag, Database diag. (hierarchical, relational, flat file)*

User-modify: *No.*

Limitations: *64K per open window (approx. 300-400 objects)*
192K per open window with "Big Desk" version.

REPOSITORY: *(Called Encyclopedia.) Located on the PC and optionally on the mainframe (IEW/MF). Managed by Knowledge Coordinator (written in PROLOG,) which applies over 2000 expert system rules to ensure completeness/consistency and provide real-time error checking.*

Objects: *32 object types.*

How integrated: *with graphics:*   *Automatic. Creating/changing an object in any diagram results in an immediate update in the Repository (encyclopedia) and all other diagrams.*
with mainframe: *Multiple PC encyclopedias (or parts) can be transferred to the host and intelligently consolidated.*

Control of sharing: *"Intelligent" merge of PC workstation Repositories on the PC or mainframe, resolves conflicts and ensures integrity of Repository objects when several analysts combine their work.*

Analysis reports: *Extensive reporting available on Repository contents.*

/continued

Information Engineering Workbench (IEW)

PROTOTYPING: *IEW/Design Workstation: Screen layouts can be produced but cannot be exercised. BMS and MFS screen maps can be generated as well as COBOL record descriptions for each screen.*
GAMMA: Screen and report layouts can be previewed; screen navigation can be demonstrated.

CODE GENERATION:

Design WS is integrated with the GAMMA applications generator. Data structures, screens, records, modules, databases, and action diagrams are passed to application generator to generate the entire COBOL application. Target environments: MVS, CICS, IMS/DC, DB2, IMS, IDMS, VSAM.

DOCUMENT GENERATION:

Diagrams and reports created in IEW/WS can be integrated with GEM Draw, GEM Write, and Ventura Publishing for integrated text and diagram documentation.

PROJECT MANAGEMENT SUPPORT:

IEW/Planning workstation collects properties of a PROJECT object type which include scheduled end-date, estimated man-months, estimated resource dollars, priority, ranking, return on investment, risk, status, and technical complexity.

DESIGN ASSISTANCE: *Design WS includes a Database Diagrammer for designing relational, hierarchical, and flat files.*

OTHER FEATURES: *Import/export utility allows users to interface IEW/WS encyclopedia objects with other software packages*

VENDOR DIRECTION: *Continuing development of integrated CASE tool set that supports multiple methodologies. Support for OS/2 and SAA. Complete integration with application generator.*

MARKET SHARE:

1987 sales: *Workstations: 3700 units (implies revenues in $15 million range). MF: not available.   GAMMA: not available.*

1988 sales: *Workstations: 4000 units (implies revenues in $20 million range). MF: 5 units.   GAMMA: 5 units.*

Installed base at end of 1988:   *Workstations: 10,000+ units MF: 30 units.   GAMMA: 55 units.*

1989 projected sales: *Workstations: 7000 units (implies revenues in $40 million range). MF: 30-50 units.   GAMMA: 30-50 units.*

USER GROUP: *For information, contact Diana Felde at Knowledgeware.*

A powerful IPSE (Integrated Project Support Environment) system widely used in Europe, capable of linking many workstations at different locations on-line to a central project-management oriented Repository.   Components include:

Graphics Workstation (GWS)	*AT-based, builds up diagrams, stores details in local Repository ($5000 for first copy).*
MAESTRO Basic System	*On departmental file server, allows each user to work on up to 12 documents concurrently with access to an unlimited number of other documents for information ($250,000+ depending on options).*

Runs on: *Workstation: AT*   **Vendor:**   *Softlab Inc.*
                  Central system: *Motorola 4000/5000*   *Bayside Plaza*
                                  DEC VAX   *188 The Embarcadero, 7th Fl*
                                                    San Francisco, CA 94105
                                                    415/957-9175

GRAPHICS: *On GWS*
Diagram types: *DFD (Yourdon/DeMarco and Gane/Sarson), ERD, Jackson structure chart. Action diag, Nassi-Schneiderman diag, HIPO diagram.*

User-modify: *Graphics Design Editor allows any symbols to be created. Validation rules for diagrams can be customized using PROLAN (Procedural Rule based Object-oriented language) to build tailored support for any method.*

Limitations:

REPOSITORY:
Objects: *Workstation:*   *Entities, Relationships, Attributes.   Graphical objects are generated/updated during actual diagram editing process.*
                  Controller: *Object management system (data repository).*

How integrated: *with graphics:*   *Immediate feedback on syntax errors.*
                    with central Repository: *At user option, update can be immediate or at end of session.*

Note: *Central Repository on Maestro file server can interface with Panvalet, LIBRARIAN, and other library systems, both mainframe- and PC-based.*

Control of sharing: *Sub-diagram is locked for update.*

Analysis reports: *Status of tasks.*
                    Bar charts, graphs of actual effort vs. planned effort.

/continued

MAESTRO

PROTOTYPING: *Screen designer can show layout, but cannot be exercised.*

CODE GENERATION: *Screen designer can generate MFS or BMS.*
Generate Data Division + PDL for control flow. Generate
minimal Procedure Division code.

DOCUMENT GENERATION: *Basic system has extensive documentation output.*

PROJECT MANAGEMENT SUPPORT: *User-supplied Standards manual, with task lists*
on-line. Log is kept of all changes made to
each program, so earlier versions can be
restored. Problem-tracking database; user can
ask e.g. which problems are unresolved.

DESIGN ASSISTANCE: *None embedded in the product.*

OTHER FEATURES: *Basic system supports word processing, electronic mail,*
system calendar, document mark-up.

MAESTRO-Net enables controllers at different locations to be
networked together so workstation in one city can read
document in another.

VENDOR DIRECTION: *Object level locking.*
Support for more methodologies.
(28% of W. German parent is owned by BMW.)

MARKET SHARE:

1987 sales (12 months):   *50 units (5 in US) (implying revenues in the $8 million range).*
1988 sales: *170 sites (12 in US) (implying revenues in the $60 million range).*
Installed base at end of 1988:   *Approx. 450 sites.*
1989 projected sales: *Approx. 200 sites (implying revenues in the $80 million range).*

USER GROUP: *In each European country; in US started in 1989.*

Product Summary   Meta System Tool Set

Six integrated products using mainframe PSL/PSA (Problem Statement Language/Problem Statement Analyzer) as Repository, based on software developed by ISDOS project at University of Michigan:

QuickSpec:	PC Windows-based tool for data entry and Repository review, with its own local repository; upload and download from mainframe Repository.
Structured Architect (SA):	PC-based tool for Yourdon/DeMarco DFDs, builds local Repository.
Structured Architect-Integrator (SA-I):	Runs under MVS, VM/CMS, or VAX/VMS; combines local Repositories into integrated central database.
PSL/PSA:	Runs under MVS/TSO, VM/CMS, VAX/VMS, UNIX and other platforms; provides central Repository.
Report Specification Interface (RSI):	Add-on to PSL/PSA for output reformatting, or export to other products.
View Integration System (VIS):	Add-on to RSI for data modelling and normalization.

Vendor: Meta Systems
315 E. Eisenhower Parkway, Suite 200
Ann Arbor, MI 48108
313/663-6027

Price:

QuickSpec:	$ 3500
Structured Architect:	$ 3500
SA - Integrator:	$16,000
PSL/PSA:	$55,000
Report Spec Interface:	$12,000
View Integration System:	$16,000

GRAPHICS: (On Structured Architect)
Diagram types: Yourdon/DeMarco DFD.
User-modify: Yes, renaming of objects for data entry, analyses, and reporting. Entity, relationship information, process logic, data element details, etc. are entered as text thru SAs Encyclopedia Editor.

REPOSITORY: PSL/PSA can be customized to support any given set of objects and relationships.
Objects: SA: Datastore, data flow, element process, functional primitive, external.
PSL/PSA: Attribute, condition, element, entity, event, group, input, interface, memo, output, process, processor, relation, requirement, resource, set, subtype, system-parameter, unit.

/continued

Meta System Tool Set

How integrated: *with graphics:*   *Automatic creation of entry in local Repository when entered on screen.*

     with data entry: *Language is automatically translated from familiar terms to PSL terms and entered into the PSA Repository.*

     with mainframe: *SA-I combines workstation Repository and feeds into PSL/PSA.*

Control of sharing: *Through SA-I. If two workstations submit entries that would cause a conflict, SA-I sends both workstations a message; the analysts are then responsible for resolving the conflict.*

Analysis reports: *SA:*   *Subset of PSL/PSA reports.*

     PSL/PSA: *Wide variety of consistency/completeness analyses: Dictionary, List, Outline, Matrix, Pictorial, Plotted, etc.*

     RSI: *Can produce custom reports.*

PROTOTYPING:
Not explicitly supported.

CODE GENERATION:
Export data structures and other information (e.g. screens & layouts) to other products with RSI; can create 01s.

DOCUMENT GENERATION:
With RSI, or with PSL/PSA Quick Doc facility. Templates for DOD-STD-2167a documentation can be obtained as part of training/consulting effort.

PROJECT MGMT SUPPORT:
PSL/PSA tracks responsibility for items. Some configuration management capabilities (e.g. date of update) can be included in the Repository.

DESIGN ASSISTANCE:
VIS helps with normalization.

OTHER FEATURES:
Also offers Reverse Engineering Service through subcontractor. Once parser is set for a given installation's standards, it can be purchased.

VENDOR DIRECTION:
Meta Systems concentrates on systems integrators where need is for control of complex projects.

MARKET SHARE:
1987 sales: *100 units of whole Meta tool set (or parts) (implying revenues of approx. $3 million).*

1988 sales: *Approx. 200 units (implying revenues of approx. $5 million).*

Installed base at end of 1988:   *Approx. 500 installations.*

1989 projected sales: *150 installations (implying revenues of approx. $5 million).*

USER GROUP:
CASE Studies Conference and regional users group meetings. For information, contact Rebecca Sizemore at Meta Systems.

MULTI/CAM

MULTI/CAM provides a mainframe-based project management support system, integrating PC workstations running EXCELERATOR (licensed by AGS).

Runs on:	PC Workstation: XT, AT, PS/2	**Vendor:**	AGS Management Systems
			880 First Avenue
Min. PC config.:	640K, 10 Mb, mouse, EGA		King of Prussia, PA 19406
Price:	$97,000 inc. 5 workstations		215/265-1550
	$3800 for each additional workstation		

GRAPHICS:

Diagram types: Same as EXCELERATOR.

DFD, ERD/Data model diag, Structure chart/structure diagram, Document graph, Presentation diag, State-transition diagram (RTS), Matrix graph (RTS).

User-modify: With CUSTOMIZER.

Limitations:

REPOSITORY:

Objects:	PC:	All the data can be stored on the PC or on the IBM mainframe.
	Mainframe:	Project Library.

How integrated: Transparent connection to the mainframe with COAX on PC.

Control of sharing: Only the owner of the data in the project library can update it.

Analysis reports: A complete set of Extended Analysis Reports are provided with the system.

PROTOTYPING: Both screens and reports.

CODE GENERATION: Store data structures and screen maps in Project Library. Use bridges to TELON and other code generators.

/continued

198

DOCUMENT GENERATION: *All development documents automatically assembled and printed at workstation on dot-matrix or laser printer.*

PROJECT MGMT SUPPORT:

Task descriptions: *(Vendor provides SDM/STRUCTURED Standard methodologies; user can insert own tasks.)*

Checklists and worksheets.
Estimating guidelines.
Automated resource scheduling and tracking.

DESIGN ASSISTANCE: *Through the integrated methodology.*

OTHER FEATURES: *Electronic mail between workstations.   On-line tutorial on system development techniques.*

VENDOR DIRECTION:

MARKET SHARE:

1987 sales: *480 workstations at 14 sites (implying revenues of approx. $1.75 million).*

1988 sales: *300 workstations ($2.1 million).*

Installed base at end of 1988:   *650 workstations.*

1989 projected sales: *$3.5 million.*

USER GROUP: *Yes.*

Product Summary   ProKit*WORKBENCH

ProKit*WORKBENCH is a powerful PC-based product, supporting Structured Systems Engineering.

Runs on:	*XT/AT, PS/2 All models*	**Vendor:**	*McDonnell Douglas*
Min. config.:	*640K + 512K Expanded memory,*		*Dept. L863, Bldg. 280-2*
	20 Mb, mouse, CGA		*P.O. Box 516*
Price:	*$9200 for first copy*		*St. Louis, MO 63166*
			800/325-1087

GRAPHICS:

Diagram types: *DFD (Gane/Sarson notation), ERD (Chen and Bachman notations), Design DFD, Structure chart.*

User-modify: *No.*

Limitations: *800 symbols per diagram, plotted on 36" x 48", 4 levels of explosion of DFDs.*

REPOSITORY:

Objects: *(18) Data Element, Data Structure, Data Type, Data Flow, Data Store, Glossary Item, Process, External Entity, Keyboard, Configuration, State, Data Entity, Relationship, Subsystem, Design Unit, Module, Database/file.*

How integrated: *with graphics:*   *Automatic Repository update as object entered in diagram; change made to a dictionary entry is automatically reflected on all relevant diagrams.*
       with mainframe: *Import/Export utilities handle ASCII files in specified format.*

Control of sharing: *An object can be updated only on the workstation which created it, unless the sub-diagram which contains it has been checked out for update to another workstation. Subdiagram is then locked until update copy is checked back in.*

Analysis reports: *Many standard reports. Users can specify parameters (e.g. what to search on, what objects to include) to create customized reports.*

/continued

ProKit*WORKBENCH

PROTOTYPING: *Image Painter builds screens, menus, reports, forms; an existing data structure can be accessed in a pop-up window for placement e.g. of elements on screen.*
State Specification facility sets up screen-to-screen flows. On-line help panels can be included in prototype.

CODE GENERATION: *Screen/Report images can be generated in ADA, Assembler, BASIC, C, COBOL, FORTRAN, PASCAL.*
Interface available to TELON and TRANSFORM code generators and to McDonnell Douglas ProIV Application Generator.

DOCUMENT GENERATION: *None apart from dictionary analysis reports.*

PROJECT MGMT SUPPORT: *None explicit.*

DESIGN ASSISTANCE: *None explicit.*

OTHER FEATURES: *Up to 8 versions of any project can be stored.*

VENDOR DIRECTION: *Multi-user on LAN (Novell, 3-COM, IBM Token Ring), locking at object level.*
PostScript output.
BMS, MFS support.
SQL query language for Repository.
Diagram merge facility.
Support for strong data-typing.
More levels of DFD explosion.
Reverse engineering capability.
Support for project planning and on-line task lists.

MARKET SHARE:

1987 sales (4 months):	*Approx. 400 units (implying revenues of approx. $2 to 3 million).*
1988 sales:	*1000 units (implying revenues of approx. $5 to 7 million).*
Installed base at end of 1988:	*1400 units.*
1989 projected sales:	*1500 units (implying revenues of approx. $7 to 9 million).*

USER GROUP: *STRUGL (STRADIS User Group Liaison).*

A family of nine products, supporting analysis through to code generation in C, PASCAL, or ADA:

ProMod/SA: *(Structured Analysis) Supports Yourdon/DeMarco SA.*
($3995 for 1st copy on PC up to $23,960 for VAX/8xxx license.)

ProMod/RT: *(Real Time) Supports Boeing/Hatley/Pirbhai extensions to Yourdon/DeMarco for analysis of real-time systems.*
($3995 for 1st copy on PC up to $31,960 for VAX/8xxx license.)

ProMod/MD: *(Modular Design) Helps automated transition from a structured analysis model to a modular design specification by taking the output of SA or RT and producing a suggested control hierarchy of subsystems, modules, and functions, with strong emphasis on information hiding and data typing.*
($3495 for 1st copy on PC up to $27,960 for VAX/8xxx license.)

ProMod/DC: *(Design Charts) Optional add-on to MD for automatically drawing structure charts from design data.*
($500 for 1st copy on PC up to $1000 for VAX/8xxx license.)

ProMod/TMS: *(Traceability Matrix System) Optional add-on to SA, RT, and MD for producing a traceability matrix; user specifies items to be traced (e.g. a data element) and TMS produces reports listing all the places in the analysis and design details where those items are to be found.*
($500 for 1st copy on PC up to $4000 for VAX/8xxx license.)

ProMod/CM: *(Configuration Manager) Compares current development database against baselines contained in DEC/CMS and reports all changes, additions, and deletions.*
(Not available on PC: $1000 - $4000 on VAX.)

Pro/Source: *(Code Generator) Takes output of ProMod/MD and translates everything possible from the modular design into syntactically correct ADA, C, or PASCAL.*
($1495 for 1st copy on PC up to $4995 for VAX/8xxx license.)

ProCap: *(Code/Design Maintenance) Editor and interactive syntax checker for ADA, C, and PASCAL source code; also handles language-specific PDL and generates documentation.*
($995 for 1st copy on PC up to $7995 for VAX/8xxx license.)

Re/Source: *Takes existing ADA, C, or PASCAL code and generates design abstractions which can be fed into ProMod/MD to produce automatic design documentation.*
($1495 for 1st copy on PC up to $11,995 for VAX/8xxx license.)

ProMod

Runs on:	PC, VAX/VMS	**Vendor:**	Promod Inc.
Min. PC config.:	640K, 10 Mb, mouse, EGA or Hercules		23685 Birtcher Drive

Runs on: PC, VAX/VMS

Min. PC config.: 640K, 10 Mb, mouse, EGA or Hercules

Vendor: Promod Inc.
23685 Birtcher Drive
Lake Forest, CA 92630
714/855-3046 or 800/255-2689
In CA: 800/255-4310

GRAPHICS:

Diagram types: DFD (Yourdon/DeMarco) in ProMod/SA.
Control flow diag., state-transition diag. in ProMod/RT. Module
Networks, Function Networks, and Structure Chart in ProMod/MD.

User-modify: No.

REPOSITORY: (ProMod Project Library)

Objects: All objects in proprietary database during editing sessions and in
standard ASCII files for configuration control, data exchange,
and sharing with other tools.

Control of sharing: All data including graphics available in ASCII files for sharing
with other systems.

Analysis reports: Extensive reports in Analysis Phase, Top Level Design Phase,
and Detailed Design Phase. Also extensive program level
reports with ProCap.

PROTOTYPING: None: code is generated directly.

CODE GENERATION: Pro/Source generates ADA, C, or PASCAL code from design
information. Syntactically correct code constructs are translated
when possible; other design information is translated as design
abstractions.

DOCUMENT GENERATION: Provides technical content of 2167 reporting
requirements.

PROJECT MGMT SUPPORT: All data is date- and time- stamped and is available via
standard ASCII files for any project management system.

DESIGN ASSISTANCE: ProMod/MD suggests a modular design to implement the
system model built up with ProMod/SA or ProMod/RT based on
Parnas' concepts of information hiding and strong data typing.

VENDOR DIRECTION: Broaden platform to UNIX-based workstations. Expand support
in design. Support other languages in CAP.

Product Summary

Software through Pictures (StP)

StP is a very powerful 32-bit-workstation-based CASE environment, intended for modelling of complex systems.

Runs on:	*Sun, Apollo, VaxStation, Sony, HP9000 workstations Supports heterogenous network*	**Vendor:**	*Interactive Development Environments 595 Market Street, Suite 1200 San Francisco, CA 94105 415/543-0900*
Min. config.:	*4 Mb*		

Price:	*Structured Analysis facility:*	*$7000 for first copy*
	Structured Analysis & Design facilities combined:	*$11,000 for first copy*
	Structured Analysis & Design for Real-Time systems:	*$15,000 for first copy*
	Object-Oriented Design/Ada	*$8000 for first copy (tentative)*

GRAPHICS:

Diagram types: *DFD (Gane/Sarson and Yourdon/DeMarco notations), Data structure diag. (Jackson), ERD (Chen notation), Control flow diag., State-transition diag., structure chart.*

User-modify: *Wide range of customization and extension options.*

Limitations:

REPOSITORY:

Uses proprietary RDBMS which is multi-user with a published schema, allowing transfer to other RDBMSs.

Objects: *All diagram objects, and the diagrams themselves. All objects and their properties are stored in Repository.*

How integrated:	*with graphics:*	*User issues command (mouse click) to update Repository.*
	with mainframe:	*Import/Export.*

Control of sharing: *Diagram locked for update. Manual locking by project administration is also available.*

Analysis reports: *Extensive. 50+ templates supplied for standard reports with outputs to ASCII, PostScript, Interleaf, Device-Independent TROFF. Template language supports customization of reports and definition of new ones.*

PROTOTYPING:

RAPID/USE facility enables exercising of screens.

/continued

204

Software through Pictures (StP)

CODE GENERATION: *Generates data declarations in C, Ada, and PASCAL. Generates database definitions for SQL-based RDBMSs such as ORACLE.*

DOCUMENT GENERATION: *Template definition language allows document structure to be specified. Interface to desktop publishing packages such as Interleaf and Frame.*

PROJECT MANAGEMENT SUPPORT: *Integration with version control and configuration management systems available from workstation vendors and third parties.*

DESIGN ASSISTANCE: *Design metrics report available as standard template.*

OTHER FEATURES: *2-D object-oriented drawing tool, Picture.*

VENDOR DIRECTION: *Provide SQL query capability for Repository. Support SADT/IDEF. Object-oriented development process, with OO analysis and design methods and tools, and code generation for Ada, C, C++, etc. Link to code generators and compilers; develop integrated CASE product. Distributed CASE, using X Windows servers and clients.*

MARKET SHARE:

1987 sales:	*300 units (implying revenues of approx. $2 million).*
1988 projected sales:	*700 units (implying revenues of approx. $6 million).*
Installed base at end of 1988:	*1200 copies at 200 sites.*
1989 projected sales:	*Not available but thought to be 1000 to 1500 units (implying revenues in $15 million range).*

USER GROUP: *First meeting, March 1988. Development Partner program involving key users.*

Software through Pictures is a trademark of Interactive Development Environments, Inc.

SYSTEM ENGINEER

LBMS SYSTEM ENGINEER (formerly known as AUTOMATE) is a multi-level product capable of running a standalone or in a multi-user environment. It is developed and marketed by LBMS of the US and UK. It has extensive graphical modelling capabilities integrated with a central repository which may reside on the PC or on a central network server. Prototyping facilities include screen painting, and walkthrough of the screens in the sequence designed.

Runs on:	AT, PS/2, or any IBM compatible	**Vendor:**	LBMS
Min. config.:	640K, 40Mb Hard Disk, 4Mb expanded memory, Microsoft Windows, mouse, CGA		2900 North Loop West, Suite 800 Houston, TX 77092 800/231-7515
Price:	$7500 for first copy.		

GRAPHICS: Intelligent Diagram Editor checks rules and consistency.

Diagram types: 18 different diagram types, including:

Method specific diagrams:	Entity Models, DFDs, Menu Dialog Structure, Transaction Dialog Structure, Entity Life History diags, Module Sequence Maps, DB2 table diag, ADABAS file diag, ORACLE table diag, Bachman (IDMS) record diag.
Generic diagrams:	Structure charts, decomposition diags, program flow charts, program structure charts, batch run flows, presentation graphics, Yourdon-style DFDs, including full functional decomposition, and Chen-style ERD.

User-modify: No.

Limitations: None.

REPOSITORY:

Objects: All diagram, prototype, and design objects.

How integrated: Interactive graphics/repository. Immediate validation, consistency checking, etc. Full support of EDIF (Electronic Data Interchange Format) for generic import/export. Hard interfaces to IDD, Predict, and DATAMANAGER dictionaries.

Control of sharing: Full multi-user version on a central server on Local Area Network, with object level locking. Password check-in/out of central server.

Analysis reports: Standard reports as well as user-defined reports can be generated by querying the database/dictionary.

PROTOTYPING:

Screen/Report Painting includes selecting data items from data inventory, and logical or physical data model. Linked with the Dialog Tester, the designer can walk through the prototype screens in the sequence defined by the dialog diagrams. The prototype can be transformed into a system skeleton, which becomes the framework for systems design.

/continued

SYSTEM ENGINEER

CODE GENERATION:
> Can generate pseudo-code from the data model, which can then be fed to backend code generators. Currently available are interfaces to Sage Software's APS Integrator and Pansophic's Telon. Automatically generates the Database Definition Statements for DB2, ADABAS, ORACLE, and IDMS.

DOCUMENT GENERATION:
> A full reporting system with a great deal of user selectivity, including specification of front and title pages as well as contents lists. Postscript, Ventura interfaces.

PROJECT MGMT SUPPORT:
> Bridge to Princeton Management Services project management software.

DESIGN ASSISTANCE:
> *Data Design:* Full entity/relationship data modelling facilities as well as intelligent interactive normalization. Physical Database Design is also done automatically for DB2, ADABAS, ORACLE, or IDMS.
>
> *Process design:* Generic "system design language" is generated from the transactions identified in prototyping and the data model. The "system design language" fills out the system skeleton, ready for export to code generators.

OTHER FEATURES:
> Full central server-based, multiuser capabilities with full record locking and control via 3COM, Novell, and IBM Token Ring. Interface to LBMS Strategic Planner.

VENDOR DIRECTION:
> OS/2 & Presentation Manager.
> Support of Mainframe Repositories.
> Reverse Engineering.
> Interface to LBMS Project Manager software, with estimating and object checking.
> Object-oriented Design.
> Object Library for reusability.

MARKET SHARE:

1987 sales (12 months):	1750 units (implying product revenues of approx. $4 million).
1988 sales:	Approx. 2000 units (implying revenues of approx. $5 million).
Installed base at end 1988:	4000 units.
1989 projected sales:	Not available, but thought to be in $10 million range. (In addition to these figures, LBMS has substantial consulting business.)

USER GROUP: European Group formed 5 years ago; meets three times annually in London, England. US group in formation. For information, call 800-231-7515.

Product Summary   TEAMWORK Family

A powerful family of products supporting Yourdon/DeMarco structured analysis and design, running primarily on 32-bit workstations. (Only TEAMWORK/PCSA runs on the PC.)

TEAMWORK/PCSA	*Supports DFDs, process specifications, structure chart, builds data dictionary. Can transfer to/from other TEAMWORK products via an Electronic Design Interchange Format (EDIF) file. Can provide PostScript output. ($995 for first copy.)*

The workstation tools can be used singly or in combination, all interacting with common Project Databases.

TEAMWORK/SA	*Supports DFDs, process specifications. ($7500 for first copy.)*
TEAMWORK/RT	*Supports unified Control Flow/Data Flow diag, Matrix diag, State transition diag, Decision table, Process Activation table, for modelling real-time systems. ($7500 for first copy.)*
TEAMWORK/IM	*Supports ERD (Chen notation). ($7500 for first copy.)*
TEAMWORK/SD	*Supports structure charts, windows to display data structures, module specifications. Maintains multiple versions of design. ($7500 for first copy.)*
TEAMWORK/IPSE	*Environment for integrating TEAMWORK with other CASE tools and custom software. ($900 for first copy.)*
TEAMWORK/DPI	*Accesses TEAMWORK Project Library to create input to external Document Production Systems WPS/TPS (Interleaf), PicED (Context), Scribe (UNILOGIC), which in turn produce documentation in various formats (e.g. DoD-STD-2167).*
TEAMWORK/MCM	*Model Configuration Management. Supports Version Control.*
TEAMWORK/ADA	*Generates ADA code. ($7500 for first copy.)*
TEAMWORK/ACCESS	*User interface to Project Library for custom reports or to generate database definitions, input to code generators, etc. ($900 for first copy.)*

Runs on: *PCSA: XT, AT, PS/2*   **Vendor:**   *CADRE Technologies Inc.*
          Others: All Apollo workstations,   222 Richmond Street
                    DEC VAXstation II, IBM PS/2   Providence, RI 02903
                    RT-PC, SUN-3, SUN-2   401/351-CASE
Min. PC config.: *512K, 2 floppies, mouse, CGA*

/continued

TEAMWORK

GRAPHICS:
Diagram types: *See opposite page.*
User-modify: *No.*

REPOSITORY:
Objects: *All diagram objects, graphics, and text.*

How integrated: *With graphics: automatic when object entered on screen.*

Control of sharing: *Workstation DBMS (e.g. Apollo's D3M, Sun's UNIFY) controls locking for update. Only one person can update the model at a given time. Check-out subsections.*

Analysis reports: *Extensive, with TEAMWORK/ACCESS.*

PROTOTYPING: *None.*

CODE GENERATION: *None explicit. TEAMWORK/ACCESS can generate database definitions.*

DOCUMENT GENERATION: *TW/DPI.*

PROJECT MGMT SUPPORT: *Status sheet keeps track of ownership, last update, planned completion date, and other management information.*

DESIGN ASSISTANCE: *None explicit.*

OTHER FEATURES:

VENDOR DIRECTION: *Pansophic Systems purchased 8% of CADRE in October 1987. Pansophic is working to incorporate TEAMWORK with TELON. A VAR agreement exists with Relational Technology Inc. to integrate TEAMWORK tightly with INGRES.*

MARKET SHARE:

1987 sales: *1000 installations (implying sales in the $10 million range).*
1988 sales: *2000 installations (implying sales in the $20 million range).*
Installed base at end of 1988:   *4000 installations.*
1989 projected sales: *4000 installations (implying sales in the $40 million range).*

USER GROUP: *For information, contact Karen Chiacu at CADRE.*

Product Summary   # TELON

TELON provides a powerful application development tool by combining the structured analysis and design capability of TEAMWORK under OS/2 with the prototyping, generation, and testing capabilities of TELON. The application developer uses diagrams to describe the business need and the architecture of the MIS solution. This information automatically feeds the TELON generator, creating complete application systems in COBOL or PL/I for IMS, CICS, or DB2 environments.

Runs on: *TSO/CICS*   **Vendor:**   *Pansophic Systems Inc.*
                                                           2400 Cabot Drive
Price: *$130,000 - $300,000*   *Lisle, IL 60532*
Latest release: *2.0*   *312/505-6000*
                                                           800/323-7335

COMPONENTS:

TEAMWORK/IM	See TEAMWORK product description
TEAMWORK ISA	on preceding pages. TEAMWORK is
TEAMWORK/SD	available from Pansophic as well as
TEAMWORK/Access	from CADRE.
TELON Design Facility (TDF)	

Programmer specifies:

Panel Image:	*location of literals and data areas on a screen.*
Panel Definition:	*the source/destination of data, field attributes, edit criteria, etc.*
Screen Definition:	*cursor positioning, screen-to-screen flow, data access, PF key processing, custom code to be included.*
Application Generator:	*Takes the files created by TDF and generates COBOL or PL/I code to run under CICS, IMS, or TSO.*
	All programs use a standard hierarchical structure.
TELON Test Facility:	*Interactive debugging tool; can test a whole application or just one screen on its own. Full-screen trace of every database access.*

GRAPHICS:
Diagram types:

	In TELON:	*Screen and report layouts*
	In TEAMWORK:	*Entity Relationship Diagram, Data Flow Diagram, Process Specifications, Structure Charts, Module Specifications, State Transition Diagrams.*

/continued

TELON

REPOSITORY:

Objects: *VSAM files containing Panel Definition and Screen Definition data.*

Control of sharing: *Components are locked when in use.*

Analysis reports: *Reports showing where custom code is used, how databases are accessed, where data elements are used.*
Diagrams.
Consistency and completeness reports.

PROTOTYPING: *TDF contains a Prototyping Facility for displaying screens, exercising edits, and showing screen-to-screen flow.*

CODE GENERATION: *Generate COBOL or PL/I for batch, IMS/DC, CICS environments accessing DL/1, DB2, or VSAM.*

DOCUMENT GENERATION: *None apart from analysis reports.*

PROJECT MGMT SUPPORT: *None explicit.*

DESIGN ASSISTANCE: *Automated enforcement of structured analysis and design techniques (through TEAMWORK).*

OTHER FEATURES: *Interface to PANVALET.*

VENDOR DIRECTION: *Pansophic acquired 8% of CADRE Technologies (see TEAMWORK) in October 87. Open architecture is supported through the published TELON Transport Facility, available for interfacing other tools with TELON.*

MARKET SHARE:

1987 sales: *71 installations (implying revenues of approx. $13 million).*
1988 sales: *Approx. 90 installations (implying revenues of approx. $15 to 20 million).*
Installed base at end 1988:   *Approx. 370 installations.*
1989 projected sales: *Not available. Thought to be 100 to 120 installations (implies sales in $20 million range).*

USER GROUP: *Annual meetings. Contact Pansophic for further information.*

A family of mainframe-based application generators using expert system technology to generate COBOL code for MVS batch, IMS, CICS, or DB2 environments.

Transform/Batch:	*($43,500 - $65,000)*	*Generates standard COBOL or COBOL II.*
Transform/IMS:	*($149,000 - $295,000)*	*Generates standard COBOL or COBOL II.*
Transform/CICS:	*($149,000 - $225,000)*	*Generates COBOL II.*
Transform/DB2:	*($50,000 - $75,000)*	*Generates standard COBOL or COBOL II.*

Each product has two main components:

Schema Management System (SMS) enables the analyst to define data screen layouts, screen-to-screen flow, and processing logic, all of which is stored in an Active Data Dictionary (Definition Database).

Application Management System (AMS) analyzes all application specifications on the Definition Database to generate COBOL code, screen maps, database definitions, program specification blocks, documentation, and JCL. All application components are compiled and link-edited without user intervention.

Maintenance is accomplished by changing SMS definitions (application specifications). AMS will then ensure that all relevant changes are made to all impacted application components (programs, screens, databases, etc.).

Runs on: *CICS or IMS/DC*   **Vendor:**   *Transform Logic Corporation*
8502 East Via de Ventura
Scottsdale, AZ 85258
602/948-2600

GRAPHICS: *Interface/TLC. Analyst defines application using pop-down windows and point-and-select with a mouse.*
Pro*Kit from McDonnell Douglas. Provide design and component specification which may be uploaded to Transform's active data dictionary.
PC Link ($6,700 - $10,000) provides capability to upload from EXCELERATOR and other modelling tools.

REPOSITORY: *(Referred to as the Definition Database.) A DL/1 database or VSAM file managed by Schema Management System (SMS).*

Objects: *Fields, Relations, Databases, User views, Screen Painter, Transactions, Table Look-up Modules, User Security, Terminals, Menus, and PF Key Sets.*

/continued

TRANSFORM

How integrated: *With graphics: Visual Software, Pro*Kit, and EXCELERATOR.*
Complete application integration with Schema Management
System/Application Management System and PC Access.
Fully automated environmental migration capabilities for movement of
schema specifications, source and load modules from development to
production environments.

Control of sharing: *Via DL/1 or DB2 locking.*

Analysis reports: *Extensive impact analysis, generation and implementation reporting*
capability.   Full environmental migration reporting.

PROTOTYPING: *PROTOTYPER option ($8,500 - $12,500) simulates defined screens,*
screen actions, and screen PF key switching activities, without the
overhead of actual application/code generation.

CODE GENERATION: *Application Management System (expert system with over*
200,000 rules) analyzes Repository and generates COBOL
source code.   The programmer can create handwritten COBOL
code modules (e.g. for complex formulas), which TRANSFORM
will include in-line in generated application.

DOCUMENT GENERATION: *User-generated, accessing DL/1 database.*

PROJECT MGMT SUPPORT: *SMS maintains multiple versions of definitions and may*
recall and implement them at any version level.

DESIGN ASSISTANCE: *Using above-mentioned design front-end tools.*

OTHER FEATURES: *11-minute videotape available on functionality and benefits.*

VENDOR DIRECTION: *OS/2 Workstation*
DB2 Repository
Reverse engineering

MARKET SHARE:

1987 sales (12 months):   *10 units (implying revenues of approx. $5 million).*
1988 sales: *12 units (implying revenues of approx. $5 million).*
Installed base at end of 1988:   *52 sites.*
1989 projected sales: *20 units (implying revenues in $15 million range).*

USER GROUP: *National Transform Users Group; also Regional Users Groups.*
For more information, contact Sharon Allen at Transform.

Visible Analyst Workbench (VAW)

VAW is a relatively low-cost modular, PC-based product with four components:

Visible Analyst: *(Tool A)*	*builds up free-form diagrams, using 21 pre-programmed DFD and flowchart symbols, with the ability to generate and use your own symbols.*
Visible Rules: *(Tool B)*	*analyzes a DFD or set of DFDs produced with Visible Analyst, and generates error messages if it does not conform to the syntax of the Yourdon/DeMarco or Gane/Sarson technique.*
Visible Dictionary: *(Tool C)*	*integrated with Visible Analyst and Visible Rules, automatically creates entries for each DFD object and dataflow, and enables details to be stored and listed.*
Visible Prototyper: *(Tool D)*	*paints screens (panels) using data elements from Visible Dictionary, links panels together to simulate system operation.*

Tool A is available separately, or Tools A+B, or Tools A+B+C, or Tools A+B+C+D. The contents of the Repository can be exported as an ASCII file.

Runs on:	*XT/AT/386/PS-2*	**Vendor:**	*Visible Systems Corp.*
Min. config.:	*512K, 10 Mb, mouse, CGA*		*49 Lexington Street*
	LAN version: Novell netware.		*Newton, MA 02165*
Price:	*$595 for each tool*		*617/969-4405*
	($2380 for all 4)		

GRAPHICS:

Diagram types: *DFD (Yourdon/DeMarco and Gane/Sarson). Structure chart, Data model, State-transition diagram. Free form diagrams (no syntax checking).*

User-modify: *Can add up to 40 user-created symbols, made out of any combination of lines, arcs, boxes, and shading.*

Limitations: *Max diag size 11" x 15." Hercules supported but no EGA.*

REPOSITORY:

Objects: *Data Element, Data flow, File, Data Store, Data Structure, External entity, Source/Sink, Process, Alias, Miscellaneous*

How integrated: *with graphics:*   *entry automatically created for each DFD object or data flow.*

               with mainframe: *export Repository as ASCII file, import correctly formatted ASCII file.*

/continued

Visible Analyst
Workbench (VAW)

Control of sharing: *Networkable version has record locking; analysis can be over entire multi-user projects. Data dictionary is multi-user and interactive. Multiple security levels supported. On-line messaging supports analyst communication.*

Analysis reports: *ANALYZE command checks syntax of DFDs on-line. Repository contents can be listed with wildcard name selection. Multiple repository analysis reports.*

PROTOTYPING: *Visible Prototyper paints screens (panels), links them with optional branching based on field entry values. Prototype can be executed with user-entered data.*

CODE GENERATION: *None.*

DOCUMENT GENERATION: *None other than diagrams and Repository listings. Pixel-to-pixel mapping technique takes maximum advantage of standard printer drivers. Presentation print outputs to 180 x 180 dpi.*

PROJECT MANAGEMENT SUPPORT: *User information maintained for each project.*

DESIGN ASSISTANCE: *None.*

OTHER FEATURES: *Multiple Security levels.*

VENDOR DIRECTION: *Bridge to industry-standard code generators.*

MARKET SHARE:

1987 sales:	*2300 units (implying revenues of approx. $4.1 million).*
1988 sales:	*4000 units (implying revenues of approx. $7 million).*
Installed base at end of 1988:	*6300 copies.*
1989 projected sales:	*8000 units (implying revenues in the $15 million range).*

USER GROUP: *None.*

Product Summary　　　　　　　　　　　**vsDesigner**

A highly-customizable PC-based modelling tool, with flexible, fully networked Repository.

Runs on:	*AT, PS/2*	**Vendor:**	*Visual Software Inc.*
Min. config.:	*640K, 10Mb, mouse, EGA*		*3945 Freedom Circle, Suite 540*
Price:	*$8,500 for first copy.*		*Santa Clara, CA 95054*
	$3,500 for non-networked		*408/988-7575*
	vsVision product		

GRAPHICS:

Diagram types: *vsDesigner is methodology independent. Its default design syntaxes are DFD (Yourdon/DeMarco and Gane/Sarson), Warnier Orr diag, Process flow diag, Action diag, Booch diag, Structure chart, Visual RT (real-time) diag, Ward-Mellor, Visual vsDraw.*

User-modify: *vsObject Maker ($3995) enables customization of objects, validation rules, and object attributes.*

Limitations: *Objects can be in color, fixed-sized, text-sized, user-sized, contain multiple labels (each with its own data dictionary entry). Connectors can be in color, solid or dashed lines, right-angled, free-angled, or arced with any graphic object as an endpoint. Up to 16K per object in data dictionary.*

REPOSITORY:

Objects: *Global attributes (an encyclopeida shared among different objects), object attributes (associated with a particular instance of an object). Four types of text (documentation, code, design reviews, and a to-do list/notepad).*

How integrated:　　　　*with graphics:　　immediate update on changing diag.*
　　　　　　　　　　　　　　with mainframe:　　immediate update on changing diag.

Control of sharing: *Node level locking of objects. Full LAN-shared access to Repository.*

Analysis reports: *vsSQL ($1995) allows user-defined queries of Repository. Library of predefined queries provided (e.g. management reports and advanced analysis).*

/continued

216

vsDesigner

PROTOTYPING: *"System Modelling" is supported for on-line systems. Support for text-based and/or icon-based systems. Users see prototypes of system screens.*

CODE GENERATION: *Code frame generation is supported with error checking (syntax, reserved works, etc.). Conforms to SAA, ANSI 85, and Microfocus specs. "Code" text objects are automatically inserted into the code frames for a very high percentage of total system being generated.*

DOCUMENT GENERATION: *Design report can include all diagrams and associated text. Facility to emulate commands of Multimate, MS-WORD, Wordstar, Wordperfect, and other word processors. Dot-matrix, HP Laserjet, and plotters supported. Facility for interfacing to Ventura Publisher and Postscript.*

PROJECT MGMT SUPPORT: *Object attributes include estimated man-hours, percentage complete, due-date, and critical issues, and can be queried with SQL (some standard queries are provided). Interfaces to Timeline and Harvard Project Manager.*

DESIGN ASSISTANCE: *In multi-tasking or networked configurations, a user-defined "design QA engine" can run in the background or on a dedicated workstation and check the quality of the design.*

OTHER FEATURES: *Strategic planning via vsSQL analysis program.*

VENDOR DIRECTION: *Continued OS/2, SAA support.*
Interfaces to strategic products defined in IBM CASE environment.
Logical validation.

MARKET SHARE:

1987 sales (6 months):   *550 units (implying revenues of approx. $2.75 million).*
1988 sales: *$5 million.*
Installed base at end of 1988: *Approx. 1500 units.*
1989 projected sales: *$10 to 12 million.*

USER GROUP: *Yes. 24-hour bulletin board system available.*

CASE products not covered in this report for various reasons (such as difficulty in acquiring current information) include:

Products	Vendor	Address/phone
Case/Pac	On-Line Software	2 Executive Drive Fort Lee, NJ 07024 201/592-0009
DesignAid	Nastec Corp.	24681 Northwestern Hwy. Southfield, MI 48075 313/353-3300
DesignMachine	Ken Orr & Assoc.	1725 Gage Blvd. Topeka, KS 66604 913/273-0653
managerVIEW	MSP	131 Hartwell Avenue Lexington, MA 02173 617/863-5800
Pacbase	CGI Systems	1 Blue Hill Plaza Pearl River, NY 10965 914/735-5030

INDEX